WARFARE IN ANCIENT GREECE

Text by
NICHOLAS VICTOR SEKUNDA
Colour plates by
ANGUS McBRIDE

First published in Great Britain in 1986 by
Osprey Publishing, Elms Court, Chapel Way,
Botley, Oxford OX2 9LP,
United Kingdom
Email: osprey@osprey-publishing.co.uk

Also published as Elite 7 *The Ancient Greeks*

British Library Cataloguing in Publication Data

Sekunda, Nick
    The Ancient Greeks.—(Elite series; 7)
    1. Greece—Armed Forces
    I. Title   II. Series
    355′. 00938 U33

    ISBN 1-85532-936-0

Filmset in Great Britain
Printed through World Print Ltd, Hong Kong

FOR A CATALOGUE OF ALL BOOKS PUBLISHED BY
OSPREY MILITARY, AUTOMOTIVE ANDAVIATION
PLEASE WRITE TO:

The Marketing Manager, Osprey Publishing,
PO Box 140, Wellingborough,
Northants, NN8 4ZA,
United Kingdom

VISIT OSPREY'S WEBSITE AT:
http://www.osprey-publishing.co.uk

FRONT COVER: Warrior painted on a calyx-crater by the Dokimisia Painter in the 460s. (Museum of Fine Arts, Boston).

Warriors of Ancient Greece

Introduction

The subject of this book is Greek warfare in the Classical Period, which stretches from the Greek victories over the Persian Empire at the beginning of the 5th century BC to the death of Alexander the Great at the end of the 4th century. During this period we see city-states such as Athens and Sparta grow to become major world powers, challenging even the mighty Persian Empire. By the middle of the 4th century, however, inter-state warfare had weakened the Greeks to such an extent that Macedon's power grew virtually unchecked.

The main aim of this book is to give the reader as full an account as possible of Greek military dress during the period. There can be little doubt that in the Archaic period, which preceded the Classical, Greek warriors simply wore what they wanted, and military 'uniform' was unknown. During the Classical Period, however, the state began to play an increasingly important rôle in military organisation, even taking responsibility for arming and equipping its citizens, or compelling the citizens to equip themselves up to a certain standard. The result was uniformity in dress and equipment. At first the army might be distinguished by some 'field sign'—such as a helmet or a shield painted in some distinguishing colour—or by a uniform shield device. Subsequently, the state might enjoin its citizens to equip themselves in cuirasses or helmets of a certain model. Regional differences in dress and weaponry also played their part in this process. So did periodic fads in military fashion, seen most clearly in the widespread adoption of Lakonian styles of military dress by Sparta's allies during her period of supremacy. It does not seem that the majority of Greek armies entered the Peloponnesian War in uniform, but the situation had changed dramatically by the end of the war. By the middle of the 4th century uniform had become general.

The literary texts are an invaluable source of

This bronze statuette, probably of Lakonian manufacture, has been dated to the early 5th century. Our Plate A1 is based on this figure, but for the addition of the staff in his hand. The transverse crest could be a badge of rank. (Wadsworth Atheneum, Hartford, Conn.)

3

Left: Reconstruction of the standard of Athena carried in the Great Panathenaic Festival, following Svoronos. The only component of the standard recovered, on which the whole reconstruction is based, is the finial of the cross-bar: see further discussion in text. (After *Archaiologikon Deltion* 6, 1920/21, p. 46) Right: The *dokana*, or 'beams', of Castor and Pollux are shown on this Lakonian grave relief. It has been suggested that the *dokana* were carried into battle before the king. (The Archaeological Museum, Sparta, 588)

information to the archaeologist trying to reconstruct an accurate picture of military dress, but by themselves they are not sufficient. They might tell us what colour a tunic was, but they can tell us nothing of its cut, or of the appearance of the wearer's helmet, cuirass or sword. Funerary monuments are our most important source in this respect, for they tend to give quite a detailed and accurate picture of the deceased: an ancient sculptor would no more dream of showing a Spartan wearing an Attic helmet than a modern one would of showing a British paratrooper wearing an Argentinian sombrero. Sometimes, fugitive traces of the original colour may still be left on the surface of sculptures to aid our work. Vase paintings, especially Attic, are a second major source, but here we must be more careful, since most Attic vases were made for the export market and may not depict

Athenians at all. Again, it is often difficult to distinguish between fanciful mythological scenes and realistic historical depiction. As a source of information on Greek military dress in general, however, they are invaluable, and it is sad to trace the decline in the practice of figurative vase painting during the 4th century. A third major source of archaeological information is coinage, which is especially valuable when it shows shields bearing the state emblem: in these cases there is surely an indication of uniform shield designs. Finally, we have an assortment of odd terracottas, bronze figurines, weapons and other artefacts.

Chronology is of absolutely prime importance when using ancient literary or archaeological information, and information from non-contemporary sources has to be regarded with the greatest suspicion. The Roman writer Statius gives us a tableau of Greek warriors dressed in all kinds of theatrical costume. He tells us of Thebans who use the sphinx as a crest (*Thebaid* 7.252); Roman sarcophagi decorated with mythological scenes also show Theban heroes with sphinxes on their shields. It is easy to be misled by information like this. There is, for example, no contemporary evidence for military standards; though mentioned in several Latin sources, they were not used before the Hellenistic period. The Greek archaeologist Svoronos thought that a small *appliqué* showing Athena discovered on the Acropolis might have formed the terminal of the cross-bar of a *labarum* of the Athenians in the Great Panathenaic Festival. He painstakingly reconstructed the rest of the standard using comparative information. Unfortunately, there is no really firm evidence that this standard ever existed at all; and even if it did, it had no military function. In Sparta we learn that Castor and Pollux were represented by a standard known as the *dokana*; but the *dokana* seem to have had a purely religious, not military, significance.

Though the bulk of this book is devoted to a discussion of the evidence for uniform, space has also been found to include some details of military organisation and tactics. I have avoided lengthy descriptions of the battles and campaigns of the Persian and Peloponnesian Wars, which are already adequately covered in innumerable works on Greek history; but I have tried to include a little information on some military incidents which are less well known, but no less interesting for that. Further information on military equipment *per se* can be found in A. M. Snodgrass, *Arms and Armour of the Greeks* (Thames & Hudson, 1967) and in Peter Connolly's magnificently illustrated *Greece and Rome at War* (Macdonald Phoebus Ltd., 1981), both of which are available at the time of writing. Abbreviations used in this text follow those used in *The Oxford Classical Dictionary* (Oxford University Press, 1970).

Because the material which follows is closely integrated with the subjects of the colour plates, I have departed from the normal series style of isolating plates commentaries in the last chapter.

Readers will find cross-references to the plates placed progressively throughout the main text.

Hoplite Warfare

At the turn of the 5th century the Greek battlefield was dominated by the hoplite, a fully armoured spearman whose main defence was his round bronze shield. The Spartans were masters of hoplite warfare due to the strict code of Spartan upbringing—the *agōgē*. From the age of six the

Bronze statuettes of Socrates are quite common. This comic one, from Egypt, is particularly interesting as it shows the philosopher wearing his cloak in the same manner as Plate A1. (Manchester Museum, 11083)

young Spartan warrior lived in barracks, and only after the age of 30 was he able to return to normal family life. In this way military supremacy over the subordinate population was guaranteed. Sparta was the most powerful city in the state of Lakedaimon, but power was shared to some degree with the *perioikoi*, or 'those who dwell about'. The gentry of these subordinate communities were willing to support Spartan supremacy in Lakonia in return for Spartan support for their social ascendancy within their own communities. At the bottom of the ladder stood the helots: communities conquered some time in the past and reduced to serfdom.

Strictly speaking, the term Spartan or Spartiate should only be used when talking of the city of Sparta and its inhabitants. 'Lakedaimon' or 'Lakedaimonian' should be used when talking of the whole state or of its army. This usage is followed throughout the book. The term Lakonian is used of the dress, speech or other characteristics of the region of Lakonia, within which the city of Sparta and the state of Lakedaimon lay.

Plate A1: Lakedaimonian officer, *c.* 490 BC
This plate represents a Lakedaimonian magistrate or emissary abroad as he might have appeared around 490. It is based on a bronze statuette, probably of Spartan origin, now in America. Badges of rank were traditionally worn on the helmet, so the transverse crest is probably best regarded as such.

Left: Few examples survive of this rare coin, struck in Chalcis in 507. The oval Boeotian shield with its scalloped rim was now obsolete, but it continued to be used as a badge by the Boeotian League. In the centre of the shield is the initial letter *'chi'* for Chalcis. (E. Babelon, *Traité des Monnaies grecques et romaines* I, ii, 1907, nr. 1372) Right: Tetradrachm issued by Samian refugees in Zancle. Weight standard and findspots prove these coins to be of Sicilian origin. The Samians were expelled by Anaxilas, Tyrant of Rhegium, in 489. Cf. Plate A2. (British Museum)

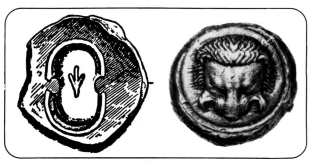

The ancient Greeks believed that the constitution of the Lakedaimonians was devised by a semi-legendary figure called Lycurgus. According to a number of ancient sources, including Xenophon (*Lac. Pol.* 11.3), Lycurgus dressed the army in crimson garments because they bore the least resemblance to women's clothing, and gave them bronze shields because bronze is very quickly polished and tarnishes very slowly. Though we may doubt that all the laws of Lycurgus are quite as old as the ancient Greeks believed, these practices must have been well established by the time of Xenophon for the soldier-historian to have believed them to have been of such antiquity. It seems probable, then, that the Lakedaimonian army was one of the first Greek armies to have adopted uniform dress, and that this practice might date back to the Archaic period.

Our figure is wearing a large cloak wrapped round the body. This cloak was probably the *tribōn*, which a number of ancient texts mention as being the distinctive mark of the Lakedaimonian. Austerity was the key-note to the Lakedaimonian life-style, and these demonstrative soldiers would emphasise their toughness by making use of a single cloak, summer and winter, allowed to wear thin and never washed. It later became popular for philosophers to ape Lakedaimonian customs, and Lakedaimonian dress in particular, by wearing single-soled Lakedaimonian sandals, the *tribōn*, and by carrying a staff. A great number of representations of Greek philosophers have survived from antiquity wearing large cloaks wrapped either completely round the body, or under the right armpit to leave the right arm free, and these serve to confirm an identification of the large cloak with the *tribōn*. There seems to be little difference, in fact, between the *tribōn* and the *himation*, a wide enveloping outer garment, which was the normal garment of the Greek gentleman in the Archaic period. In the rest of Greece, however, the *himation* was being discarded for a combination of tunic (*chitōn*) and cloak (*chlamys*), and only in conservative states like Lakedaimon did the old fashions retain their popularity.

The staff (*bakterion*) was another sign of the Lakedaimonian. Lakedaimonians abroad were recognised by their staff, and it became a sort of symbol of Spartan power. The staff could either be straight, or could have a curved crook at the top which allowed the user to place it under his left armpit and to rest his weight on it by leaning forward.

Another distinctive feature of this figure which is recognisably Lakedaimonian is the long, carefully dressed hair. Lycurgus believed that long hair made a good-looking man more handsome and an ugly man more terrifying, so adult men were allowed to grow their hair long. In times of danger they paid particular attention to their hair, and one is reminded of the way the Persians on their arrival at Thermopylae were astonished to find the Lakedaimonians combing their hair in preparation (*Hdt.* 7.208–9).

The Lakedaimonian Army

The Lakedaimonians kept their military strength and organisation as secret as possible. Little was understood of these matters by the historians of antiquity, and even less by historians of more recent date (including the present author). It seems impossible to reconstruct a sensible picture of the Spartan army without violating some piece of ancient testimony or other; but it is equally impossible to write a book on armies of Classical Greece without at least making the attempt. In what follows, therefore, I offer an outline which to me seems to make the best sense of the evidence, but of which I am by no means completely certain.

At first the warriors of Sparta were simply divided into tribal contingents, one from each of the three Dorian tribes of Hylleis, Dymanes, and Pamphyloi. At some point in time, however, probably during the enactment of the Laws of Lycurgus, the Spartan population was divided up into five villages (Limnai, Mesoa, Pitane, Konosura, Dyme) which formed administrative divisions of the state called *obai*. We find the army at an early date divided into five companies, or *lochoi*, called Aidolios, Sines, Sarinas, Ploas, and Mesoates. Given the correspondence of the number five, and of at least one of the names, it seems probable that each *lochos* was raised from one *oba*. In his description of the battle of Plataea in 479 Herodotus tells us that Amompharetos commanded the Pitanate *lochos*, and it is probable that the father of history has simply substituted the name of the *oba* for the name of the *lochos*. Herodotus (9.10, 11, 61) also tells us that the Lakedaimonians sent out a levy

This *pinax* (plaque) painted by Euthymides and inscribed 'Megacles is Fine', along with other evidence, led Smith to identify the *silen* as the shield device of the Megaclids. When Megacles was ostracised in 486 his name was erased from the plaque and the name Glaukytes substituted. See under A4. (Athens, Akropolis Museum, 1037)

of 5,000 Spartans, out of their 8,000 total of available manpower, each man accompanied by seven helots fighting as *psiloi*, or light infantry; and of 5,000 *perioikoi* equipped as hoplites accompanied by 5,000 *psiloi*. Whether the helot *psiloi* were drawn up together with the hoplites, or separately from them, is not known.

Presumably the army was divided into five *lochoi* of a thousand Spartans each, but of any lower subdivisions we are entirely ignorant. The *pentekostys* or 'fifty', which is attested in later Spartan systems of military organisation, and which presumably originally formed a component of an army arranged on a decimal system, might date back to this time, so each *lochos* may have consisted of twenty *pentekostyes*.

Plate A2: Samian hoplite, c. 490 BC

Many Greek states used standardised badges to identify their coinage, and when any coin shows a hoplite shield with the city badge used as a blazon on the shield, it is a fairly good indication that the hoplites of that city might have used the city badge as a uniform shield blazon. Most of these coins come from the 4th century and later, but a couple of examples, surprisingly, come from the turn of the fifth. One tetradrachm attributed to Chalcis in

7

Detail of a warrior on a calyx-crater in the Louvre painted by The Niobid Painter, *c.* 455–450. His shield is painted white, and bears the device of a hydra, both of which features may show him to be an Argive. The vase is thought to show Herakles and the Argonauts, so perhaps our figure is the Argonaut Idmon, though this is very uncertain. See Plate A3. (Musée du Louvre, G 341)

Euboea shows a Boeotian shield with the initial letter of Chalcis in the local alphabet, *chi*, stamped on it. The Boeotian shield, however, was the badge of the Boeotian League, and the shield on this coin simply indicates that Chalcis was in alliance with Boeotia at the time, so the evidence supplied by this coin has to be rejected.

Following the collapse of the Ionian Revolt some Samians emigrated to Zancle in Sicily, and there issued coins bearing a hoplite shield with a lion's scalp as a blazon. The lion's scalp is the badge normally found on Samian coinage, so it is quite possible that Samian hoplites used uniform shield-devices at this time, or at least that some Samian hoplites favoured the state emblem as a shield-device. If this is the case then the Samians must have been one of the first Greek states after the Lakedaimonians to institute standardised uniform. Doubtless, uniform started with common shield-devices, and at this stage did not extend as far as other items of dress and equipment. Plate A2 has been given a Corinthian helmet pushed back to give the wearer better vision, and a 'composite cuirass'; bronze greaves are also worn. A peculiar feature of this period shown on a few vase paintings is that a roll of material, rather like a garter, is worn under the bottom edge of the greave to prevent chafing.

Plate A3: Argive hoplite, early 5th Century

The only army for which we have textual evidence of uniform at such an early date, other than the Lakedaimonian, is the Argive. Attic tragedians talk of the 'white-shielded army' of the Argives as early as 467, the date when Aeschylus wrote his *Seven Against Thebes* (line 89, see also Soph. *Ant.* 106, Eur. *Phoen.* 1099, Hsych. sv. *Leukaspida*). The white shield was presumably plain, though we should note that a scholiast (that is a later commentator) on Euripides' *Phoenissae* 1135 remarks that Adrastus is given a hydra on his shield on account of his being an Argive. The hydra was a water-snake, the most famous one being that killed by Herakles at Lerna in the Argive Plain. No other details of Argive military dress are given in the ancient texts, and, unfortunately, no grave reliefs or statuettes of hoplites have yet been recovered from Argos which would allow us to make a reconstruction with any confidence. Plate A3 is based on a vase-painting which could possibly show an Argive, with a white shield and a hydra as a shield-design.

Argive Military Organisation

Various references tell us that around 418, the date of the first battle of Mantineia, the Argive army comprised five *lochoi* and was commanded by five *stratagoi*, each presumably commanding one *lochos*

(Thuc. 5.59.4, 5.72.3). It may be that the normal strength of the Argive *lochos* was a thousand, which number occurs in texts mentioning Argive forces at other times in the 5th century (Hdt. 6.92, Thuc. 1.107.5). The *lochos* may have been divided up into *pentekostyes*, for a later inscription tells us that citizens were registered under *pentekostyes* on muster-rolls kept in the temple of Apollo Lykeios. This is all very reminiscent of the possible division of the Lakedaimonian army into five *lochoi* of 20 *pentekostyes* each, but we do not know which army might have copied which. Again, like the Lakedaimonian *lochoi*, the five Argive *lochoi* do not seem to have been organised upon tribal lines, for we know of only four Argive tribes: the Hylleis, Dymanes, Pamphyloi and Hyrnathioi (R. A. Tomlinson, *Argos and the Argolid*, Routledge & Kegan Paul, 1972, pp. 175–186).

The Argive Epilektoi

Argos had once been the dominant power in the Peloponnese, but now Lakedaimon had completely taken over from her, thanks to the latter's superior

Detail from a column-crater in Berlin by The Orpheus Painter. The Thracian hat was made from a fox-scalp; the ears and eye-slits are shown quite clearly in the painting; the ear-flaps are tied up with the laces showing as a loop above the cap. The neck-flap seems to be of brightly patterned cloth. Cf. Plate B1. (West Berlin, Antikenmuseum Staatliche Museen Preussischer Kulturbesitz Berlin, 3172)

military training programme. In 421 the Argives picked out a thousand of the wealthiest and fittest of their younger citizens, freed them from all public duties, and maintained them at public expense so they could devote themselves to continuous military training and exercise. Only by having their own force permanently training under arms, it was felt, could Lakedaimonian supremacy be offset. 'The Thousand', whom Diodorus (12.75, 79, 80) calls *epilektoi* or 'picked troops', particularly distinguished themselves at the first battle of Mantineia in 418. Following the defeat of the Argives in that battle, 'The Thousand' agreed among themselves to dissolve the democracy and to take power. Their rule lasted only eight months.

'The Thousand' seem to be the earliest example of troops called *epilektoi*. Though the term is used very loosely by some historians, especially Dio-

This amphora shows a Thracian peltast in full fighting order. This seems to be the only representation of a Thracian peltast wearing a helmet; though not of the type we term 'Thracian', this is of particular interest. Note also the brace of javelins, and the good luck symbols painted on the shield. Cf. Plate B1. (Oxford, Ashmolean Museum, 1971.867)

dorus, in its strict sense *epilektoi* means citizens who are 'picked out' and given maintenance by the state to concentrate permanently on military training. *Epilektoi* became more common in the 4th century; but, as we shall see later, there was a constant danger that a permanently established body of armed citizens might want to seize power for themselves, for there was little to stop them doing so.

Plate A4: Athenian hoplite of the Alkmaionid Clan, *c.* 490 BC

Notwithstanding these few early examples of uniformity in Greek military dress, there can be little doubt that in most Greek armies the hoplite went into battle in dress and equipment of his own choosing well into the Classical period. Many factors could govern a hoplite's choice of shield device (see G.-H. Chase, 'The Shield devices of the Greeks', *Harvard Studies in Classical Philology* 13, 1902, pp. 61–127 repr. Ares Publishers, Chicago,

1979). Some shield devices had a more personal significance, however, and could make some comment on the prowess of the bearer. For example, one Sophanes of Dekeleia had an anchor as his shield device to indicate his steadfastness in the ranks (Hdt. 9.74). Cases of 'canting arms' also existed. Individuals might also bear arms which had a family significance. We are told that Alcibiades had a gold shield made for himself, bearing no family device, but instead an Eros armed with a thunderbolt (Plut. *Vit. Alcib.* 16)—which can be taken to show that family shield devices did exist in Athens. Only one Athenian family shield device can be re-created with any certainty. An ancient marginal note in a play by Aristophanes (Schol. *Lysistr.* 664) seems to tell us that the shield device of the Alkmaionid clan was *Leukopodes* or 'Whitelegs', though this interpretation of the passage is far from certain. C. T. Seltman (*Athens, its History and Coinage*, Cambridge, 1924, p. 21 seq.) identified 'Whitelegs' as being the device of a single white leg, or of the *triskeles*—three running legs conjoined in the style of the modern arms of the Isle of Man, found so frequently on Athenian vase-paintings and coinage. Seltman then went on to analyse the early coinage of Athens, dating the coins to various periods when different clans were in power. He thought the horse might be a Peisistratid device, the hind-quarters of a horse a Philaïd device, the bull's head and the knuckle-bone an Eteobutad device, and so forth. Unfortunately his dating of early Athenian coinage seems to be at fault, and all these identifications must be rejected (H. J. H. van Buchem, 'Family Coats-of-Arms in Greece?', *Classical Review* 40, 1926, pp. 181–183). Much more plausible is the attempt of H. R. W. Smith ('New Aspects of the Menon Painter', *University of California Publications in Classical Archaeology* 1, 1929, pp. 54–57) to identify the 'silen' badge[1] as the device of the Megaclids, a cadet branch of the Alkmaionid clan.

These clan shield devices would not be used by a single person, but could conceivably have been used by the whole clan. The larger Athenian clans comprised a sizeable proportion of the population of Athens. We are told that in 508 some 700 households in Athens were connected with the Alkmaionid clan. The dangerous military power

[1]From Silenus, a mythical half-man, half-beast.

held by the larger clans, fighting in the same tribal ranks when the army was drawn up for battle, was probably a major factor behind the reform of the Athenian tribal system undertaken by Cleisthenes in 508/7. Henceforward the Athenian population was divided into ten tribes (Erechtheis, Aigeis, Pandionis, Leontis, Akamantis, Oineis, Kekropis, Hippothontis, Aiantis and Antiochis). Each tribe

This warrior, painted on a calyx-crater by The Dokimasia Painter in the 460s, appears to be wearing a *perizōma*, a protective kilt of blanket-weave material, underneath the groin-flaps of his composite cuirass. Note also the padding worn beneath the greaves. Cf. Plate B2. (Boston, Museum of Fine Arts, 63.1246)

was named after a different Attic hero, and was formed from parishes, or 'demes', scattered all over Attica. In this way old tribal and clan loyalties were broken down.

Plate B: Contact with the Thracians

Following their failure to conquer Greece in the Persian Wars, the Persians withdrew from the whole of Europe. This created a vacuum of power in the northern Aegean, into which the Athenians in particular attempted to expand. Greek warfare had come to be dominated by the hoplite in full armour, and by the time of the Persian Wars cavalry and missile troops were virtually absent from the Greek battlefield. Expeditions into Thrace, however, brought the Greeks into contact with new methods of warfare which would eventually force a review of hoplite tactics and equipment. The Greeks in Thrace suffered from both the bad climate and the novel local methods of warfare. Between the Persian and Peloponnesian Wars the Athenians lost nine expeditions while trying to colonise the area of the Strymon valley.

This *lekythos* by The Oinokles Painter shows a warrior cutting off a lock of hair for a dedication. The combination of muscle-cuirass and Thracian helmet becomes very popular in the 460s. A protective apron, the *perizōma*, has been substituted for the groin-flaps normally worn beneath the cuirass. Note also the pad-strips worn beneath the greaves. Cf. Plate B2. (Cleveland Museum of Art, Ohio, The Charles W. Harkness Endowment Fund, 28.660)

Plate B1: Thracian peltast

The city-state had never evolved in Thrace, and different social conditions spawned different methods of warfare. The mainstay of any Thracian prince's army was his force of peltasts. The peltasts were javelinmen equipped with a small shield, called a *pelta* or *peltē*. This made them considerably more effective as skirmish troops than the standard Greek javelinman without a shield. Unshielded javelinmen were extremely vulnerable to a defensive barrage from archers or other javelinmen. The defending missile troops could hide behind the hoplite shield wall and, perfectly safe themselves, keep any attacking javelinmen at such a distance, for fear of incurring casualties, that the hoplite line would hardly suffer at all. Once the attacking javelinmen were given shields, however, defensive missiles could be risked with more confidence. Attackers could now advance to a distance from which the hoplite line could be engaged, and the hoplites would start to suffer casualties.

The Thracian peltast was hardly anything more than a tribesman in traditional Thracian hunting-dress. Thracian dress is described by Herodotus (7.75) and other authors. The Thracian cap was made of fox-skin. Winters in Thrace were severe, so the cap was provided with a pair of earflaps to prevent frostbite. The thick square cloak, or *zeira*, extended to the knee to keep the legs warm, and the tunic was unusually thick and long. Xenophon and the Greek mercenaries who had fought for Cyrus served in Thrace, following their return from Asia, under the Odrysian prince Seuthes. When Seuthes marched against the Thynians, 'There was much snow and such frost that the water brought in for dinner froze, as did the wine in the vessels, and the noses and ears of many of the Greeks were bitten off. Hence it became clear why the Thracians wear fox-skins on their heads and over their ears, and *chitons* not only around the trunk but also around the thighs, and *zeiras* reaching down to the feet on horseback, not *chlamydes*' (*An.* 7.4.3–4). The thick blanket-weave material from which the Thracian garments were made would itself give a little protection from spent missiles. Fur-lined fawnskin boots, laced up the front and then tied off at the top of the calf so as to let the fur lining fall down in three lappets, were distinctively Thracian. The shield would be of wood covered in hide. It was of crescent shape, a segment being cut out of the top edge to allow the peltast unobstructed vision while throwing his javelin. The front of the *peltē* would be painted with some kind of primitive good-luck symbol to ensure the warrior's safety. The most popular design was some kind of stylised face: this was probably intended to give the shield magical vision in order to watch out for hostile missiles. Representations of Thracians on Attic vases tend to show them carrying only a brace of hunting javelins, though perhaps more were carried in war. The javelins were quite long, about six feet, and were fitted with small leaf-shaped iron heads.

Plates B2, B3: Greek 'Ekdromoi'

Contact with the Thracians, both friendly and hostile, hastened changes in hoplite warfare and equipment. At first the changes were very superficial. The Thracian helmet first became popular in the 460s. It is also noticeable that eyes, which occur but rarely in archaic vase painting, now become the single most popular shield design in representations of hoplites from the middle of the 5th century onwards, probably as a result of Thracian contacts. Eventually, though, campaigning in Thrace was to have a more profound effect on tactics and consequently on equipment. To keep the peltasts at bay the youngest and fittest of the hoplites were detailed to run out of the line at a given signal, in the hope of catching and killing at least a few of the peltasts and driving the rest back. These troops were known as *ekdromoi* or 'runners-out'. Hoplites would be detailed to serve as *ekdromoi* according to age-class; thus the first ten or the first

Here a full jerkin of blanket-weave material, possibly a *spolas*, provides protection for the warrior on whom Plate B3 has been based. Squat lekythos by The Achilles Painter dating to around the 440s. Note the Thracian helmet. (New York, Metropolitan Museum of Art, 17.230.13)

15 age-classes of a particular levy might be detailed to act as *ekdromoi*. In order to enable the *ekdromoi* to catch the peltasts it became inevitable that a considerable portion of the hoplite's heavy body armour would have to be discarded. From about 440 onwards we come across increasingly numerous representations of this new kind of 'light hoplite' in Greek vase-painting and sculpture.

The cuirass and greaves were discarded, but at first the *ekdromos* was not left completely unprotected. Some hoplites had previously worn an apron of thick blanket-weave material, gaily patterned after the Thracian style, underneath the groin-flaps or *pteruges* of the cuirass. When the cuirass was discarded the apron, which was probably called a *perizōma*, was frequently retained to give at least a little protection from missiles without slowing down the *ekdromos* too much. In other cases a full tunic of similar material was worn. Originally some hoplites may have worn this thick garment as an arming-tunic comparable to the gambeson of the medieval knight. It may be the *spolas* mentioned by Xenophon, but ancient lexica indicate that the *spolas* was normally made of leather. At first it seems that only the *ekdromoi* fought in this lightened equipment, for we can deduce from a number of references that cuirasses continued to be used well into the Peloponnesian War. Eventually, though, it was found that the shield and helmet gave sufficient

Detail from a *stamnos* by Polygnotos showing Theseus fighting the Amazons. On the left, Theseus wears the protective kilt, or *perizōma*, and an early form of Boeotian helmet, complete with crest but without an indented rim. On the right, Rhoikos wears Thessalian dress. The shape of the hat foreshadows the petasos-helmet. About 445–430. Cf. Plate C1. (Oxford, Ashmolean Museum V.522)

protection, and were cheaper and more comfortable to wear than the full hoplite panoply, so lightened equipment came to be adopted by the whole army.

Plate C1: Boeotian hoplite, *c.* 440 BC

Another change we see in hoplite equipment starting around the mid-5th century is the replacement of the traditional types of close helmet with more open types, such as the Lakonian 'pilos-helmet' and the 'Boeotian' types. Both these helmet types had their origin in regional patterns of felt caps. Demosthenes (59.94) mentions that a painting of the battle of Marathon, housed in the Stoa Poikilē or 'Painted Porch' at Athens, and therefore dating to some time soon after 460, showed the Plataean contingent running to Marathon wearing Boeotian hats. Vase paintings of around that time also show warriors, some of them with Boeotian associations, wearing Boeotian hats. Some of these vase-paintings show crests, indicating a development from felt hats to bronze helmets in the same shape, towards the end of the 5th century. The Boeotian hat was rather like a large-size bowler hat in shape. The brim is always shown drooping downwards. Plate C1 is based on an Attic white-ground *lekythos* or oil flask (Athens 1761) painted in colour by the Thanatos Painter.

5th Century Cavalry

Plates C2, C3: Thessalian cavalrymen

Thessaly is composed of huge plains, unique in Greece and ideally suited for growing grain and rearing cattle. The Thessalian aristocracy grew rich on the export trade in corn and stock, and one way in which it chose to display its wealth was in keeping horses. Consequently the Thessalians were the finest horsemen in Greece, and cavalry in Thessaly retained a prime importance in battle when it had become almost obsolete throughout the rest of the Greek mainland. Thessalian riding dress was quite distinct, and adapted to the climate of the landlocked plain—very hot in summer, very cold in winter, thanks to the mountain-chains which surround it. The extravagantly wide-brimmed version of the Greek *petasos*, or sun-hat, kept out the heat and dust of the plain, while the long,

enveloping Thessalian cloak kept the wearer warm in winter but cool in summer. These two distinctive features of Thessalian dress are shown on a great number of Thessalian tombstones, and also on a certain number of Attic white-ground *lekythoi* which seem to show young Athenian aristocrats dressed after the manner of their wealthy Thessalian counterparts. No coloured tombstones of Thessalians have survived from the Classical period, but it might be legitimate to reconstruct the typical colours of Thessalian clothing from the Athenian vase paintings.

Most of these Athenian figures are dressed in hats of yellowish-tan felt and Thessalian cloaks of a dark

Relief from Phalanna, dating to about 450, showing typical Thessalian dress of wide-brimmed hat, tunic and Thessalian cloak. A brace of hunting spears is carried in the left hand. (Volos, Athanassakeion Archaeological Museum, L 372)

brownish-red colour with a broad white border, as in plate C3. This could well represent typical Thessalian dress. Plate C2, however, is reconstructed from an Athenian vase (Walter Riezler, *Weissgrundige Attische Lekythen*, Munich, 1914, pl. 95) showing a horseman in Thessalian clothing, which is as striking as it is unique in colour combination. It should be noted that the Thessalian tombstones universally show a short-sleeved tunic worn underneath the cloak, whereas the Athenian vases show the cloak worn without a tunic.

At this time the typical Greek cavalry spear was the *kamax*. The word means 'reed', and was a nickname given first to long, thin vine-poles, and then to the long, thin cavalry spears which looked like them. The *kamax* was primarily designed for use against infantry, its great length being designed to enable the horseman to 'pig-stick' enemy infantry.

The Thessalian League

Thessaly did not rely exclusively on the cavalry arm, though infantry were always of less importance because of the slow development of the city-state in that region. Thessaly was traditionally divided into four tetrarchies or 'quarters' called Thessaliotis, Phthiotis, Pelasgiotis, and Hestiaiotis. These four tetrarchies formed the Thessalian League, in whose meetings votes were allocated by tetrarchy, and whose elected head was called the *tagos*. The first *tagos* was called Aleuas the Red; and a mutilated fragment (479 ed. V. Rose) from Aristotle's lost *Constitution of the Thessalians* gives some detail of the military organisation of the

Detail from The Great Melos Amphora by The Suessula Painter, now in the Louvre (S 1677), showing a battle between gods and giants. Our figure, probably Castor or Pollux, demonstrates how the *kamax* was used against infantry, with a rapid downward thrust of the small leaf-shaped head. Cf. Plates C2, C3. (After Adolf Furtwängler *Griechische Vasenmalerei* pl. 96/7; photomontage by C. Street-Cunningham)

League, which remained in force through the Classical period, though the office of *tagos* lapsed:

> 'Aleuas the Red divided Thessaly into four Tetrarchies, and having thus divided the state, he assessed the army strength at 40 horsemen and 80 hoplites per *klēros*.'

It seems that there were 150 *klēroi*, or lots, for the total army of the League numbered 6,000 cavalry and 12,000 hoplites. Something concerning peltasts or the *peltē* follows this fragment, so it is possible that the *klēros* was also responsible for furnishing a number of peltasts. In fact the dividing line between what was a hoplite and what was a peltast seems to have been somewhat blurred in Thessaly, as we might expect in a corner of Greece which was atypical in so many other respects. Figures appear on Thessalian coins and reliefs which seem to be half-way between hoplites and peltasts in equipment, wielding javelins but using hoplite shields.

Thessaly's large army allowed her to expand at the expense of her neighbours, the surrounding perioikic communities of Magnesia, Perrhaebia, and Achaea Phthiotis. A second *tagos*, called Skopas the Old, fixed the tribute the Perioikis had to pay to the League, apparently in terms of both revenues and military contributions.

Athenian Cavalry

During the period of the Persian Wars the Athenians maintained a force of only some 300 horsemen who had little military function. During the archonate of Diphilos in 442, probably as a result of a law moved by Perikles, the cavalry corps was expanded to 1,000. Each of the ten Athenian tribes supplied a tribe (*phylē*) of cavalry commanded by a phylarch. The ten *phylai* of horse were under the command of two hipparchs, who would each command a wing of five *phylai* in battle. All these officers would be elected annually. The cavalry, like the hoplites, were not paid a regular wage, but unlike the hoplites they were given an allowance of one drachma a day for fodder in times of peace or war alike. On entering service with the cavalry the young nobleman would also be paid an establishment grant (*katastasis*) to cover the cost of his mount. The *katastasis* had to be paid back on leaving the cavalry, unless the mount had been killed on active service. To avoid fraudulent

Broken relief from Larisa dating to the last quarter of the 5th century. The long cylindrical spear-butt, though nearly erased by later damage, suggests that this Thessalian horseman carries a *kamax*, a species of long cavalry spear. Cf. Plates C2, C3. (Volos, Athanassakeion Archaeological Museum, L 393)

claiming of allowances the *dokimasia* or inspection was performed annually by the Athenian council, or *boulē*, following the election of the officers. Each rider and horse would be carefully inspected for fitness for service. Horses which failed to pass the *dokimasia* were branded on the jaw with the sign of a wheel, in order to prevent them being slipped through the *dokimasia* on a future occasion. If passed the riders names would be entered on the *sanides*, or 'chalk-boards', which would be passed on to the taxiarchs, who commanded the tribal infantry regiments. The taxiarchs would delete the names of those entered on the *sanides* from the tribal recruitment rolls, which were kept by archon year, to ensure that no-one became liable for both hoplite and cavalry service.

Plate D1: Athenian cavalryman, *c.* 440 BC

A number of Athenian reliefs show the dress of the newly expanded Athenian cavalry corps just before the start of the Peloponnesian Wars. Normal military dress is shown, however, in a number of Athenian sculptures—both private funerary monuments, and state monuments to the fallen—dating from this period. From about 440 onwards it became fashionable for the Athenian nobility to spend more and more on their tombstones. The principal funerary monument from now until 317 was the marble *lekythos* or 'oil flask'. For a long time the dead had been buried with oil flasks (for toilet purposes in the after-life), and it now became popular to demarcate the tomb plot with monumental marble *lekythoi* at the edges. These marble vases are also found in a second shape, the *loutrophoros*, which was a ritual vessel used to fill the marriage bath. These marble *lekythoi* and *loutrophoroi* were usually sculpted with a representation of the deceased in an act of daily life, and are a rich source of information about Athenian military dress and equipment in the Classical period.

Plate B1 is based on a marble *lekythos* in Athens (National Museum inv. 835). All Athenian cavalry of this period have certain features of dress in common. The tunic is a *chitoniskos*, a sleeveless tunic held up by straps over the shoulders, looking rather like a modern vest. Over this is worn a bronze muscle-cuirass which passes over the shoulders only in very narrow bands so as to allow maximum freedom of movement to the arms. The head was covered by a *petasos* of the Thessalian type, and the feet were shod in the normal thin Greek cavalry boots. On Athenian reliefs these boots are very hard to detect, as the details of strap-work etc. were normally painted in; but if the toes are not clearly shown in a relief we can be sure it is because the subject is wearing boots. Weapons were also frequently painted in. These seem to have been the *kamax*, sometimes used in conjunction with a pair of javelins, and a cavalry sabre. Where the cavalry sabre is shown on these reliefs it seems to have a hilt shaped like a bird's head. In all cases the sabre is shown sheathed, however, so it is difficult to be certain whether or not the sabre would have had a curved blade or, as is more common in this period, a straight, broad blade rather like the medieval falchion in appearance. Cloaks are not shown in reliefs before the turn of the century, so perhaps they were not worn. Military dress of this type is also worn by some of the figures on the Parthenon frieze, the majority of whom are, however, not shown wearing uniform dress. Given the uniformity of dress and equipment in these figures one is forced to ask whether the Athenian cavalry were fully uniformed with tunics of the same colour at this early stage; but the answer is probably 'no'. The similarity in the type of equipment carried seems to be explained by the law of Perikles, which must have stipulated exactly what equipment a cavalryman had to possess to pass the *dokimasia*, but this would certainly not run as far as detailing clothes to be worn. Coincidences here are probably explained by prevailing fashions. The aristocratic cavalrymen aped Lakedaimonian habits: they wore their hair long, and engaged in boxing and other gymnastic exercises. Because of these practices their detractors called them 'the folk with battered ears'.

Plate D2: Athenian cavalry recruit *c.* 430 BC

It is a great pity that we do not know more of the Athenian system of ephebic training during the 5th century. The ephebe was a young man undergoing military training; it seems that the course of training lasted two years, from 18 to 20. The first year seems to have been a basic military training course for all citizens, carried out in barracks in the Piraeus. In the second year those who were in the hoplite census class were given a further year of training in hoplite warfare, during which they manned the frontier forts guarding Attica. Those who were too poor to afford hoplite equipment—like the orator Aeschines (2.167) in his youth—were trained as peltasts, and spent their second year patrolling the countryside of Attica, from which activity they were known as *peripoloi* or 'patrollers'. Thucydides (8.92.6) also mentions some cavalry *neaniskoi*, which is a word usually used to mean an ephebe, so it may be that in their second year of military training

Coin of Larisa dating to the end of the 5th century. Hoplites of Larisa may have used the cow's hoof, symbolic of Thessalian trade in beef and livestock, as a common shield device. (British Museum)

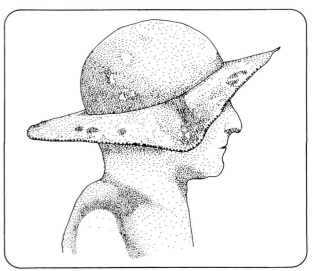

Cavalry helmet discovered in a tomb in Madytou Street, Athens. The rim is pierced all the way round the edge with a line of small holes, possibly to allow a material cover to be stitched on to the outside, thereby disguising the helmet as a hat. The total effect is very reminiscent of 17th century helmets made in hat shapes. Plate D2 wears a helmet of this type. (Drawing: Hugh Coddington)

those intending to serve in the cavalry underwent mounted training.

This brings us to Plate D2, which is based on a late 5th century Athenian white-ground *lekythos* painted by The Reed Painter (Athens, National Museum 12275). The figure of a horseman painted on it is most rare, and has a number of points of interest. First is the black *chlamys*. We know that the Athenian ephebes wore black cloaks at certain processions and festivals, so our figure may be an ephebe in training for the cavalry. Another interesting feature is the helmet in the shape of a *petasos*. It is evident on Athenian reliefs of this period that many horsemen are not wearing a *petasos*, but a metal helmet of *petasos* shape. These 'petasos-helmets' can be distinguished from a simple hat because they lie square on the brow, rather than being perched jauntily over the forehead, which is the way in which the *petasos* is normally worn. An actual example of a helmet of this type has recently been discovered in an Athenian tomb (O. Alexandri *Archaiologikē Ephēmeris*, 1973, pp. 93–105). Finally, we might note that the horseman is carrying a pair of heavy hunting spears rather than the *kamax*.

Detail from a marble *lekythos* showing a cavalryman. This is one of the earliest examples of this type of funerary monument: at this early date the *lekythoi* are very tall and thin. The style of carving is very reminiscent of the Parthenon freize, which allows us to date the sculpture to about 440. The cavalryman, on whom Plate D1 is based, wears a *petasos* hat, a thin sleeveless tunic, and a bronze muscle-cuirass. Further details, such as the spear and boot-straps, would have been painted onto the sculpture. (Athens, National Museum, 835)

The Peloponnesian War

Athenian state monument commemorating the dead of 394. The cavalryman on the right wears a petasos-helmet, or possibly an early form of Boeotian helmet. He thrusts downwards with a *kamax* and is also armed with a sabre. On the left, an Athenian hoplite with a fallen adversary. Cf. Plate D2. (Athens, National Museum, 2744)

It was probably inevitable that the rising power of Athens would eventually clash with Lakedaimon. What was perhaps not so inevitable, from a military viewpoint, was the way that the ascendancy of the hoplite, though under constant challenge during 30 years of warfare, survived the war virtually undiminished. This is not to say that hoplite armies always won—they suffered a number of defeats at the hands of peltasts or *psiloi*, frequently with the support of cavalry; but in the end the hoplite armies were able to devise new tactics to overcome their adversaries.

Greek Psiloi

It is easy for the student of Greek warfare, in devoting too much attention to the study of the peltast, to forget about the simple Greek *psilos* armed with some sort of stick or stone. Occasions did occur when even the humble rock could be used to effect against a hoplite army. In 457 the Corinthians occupied the heights of Geraneia and descended on Megara, thinking that the Athenians were too heavily committed to campaigns elsewhere. But the Athenians called out the ephebes between 18 and 20 and the old men between 50 and 60, and despatched this force under the famous general Myronides. One indecisive battle was fought; then a second one at Kimolia 12 days later. The Corinthian hoplites were thrown back, and in their confusion a considerable proportion of them lost their way and rushed into some farmland enclosed by a great ditch. It was a dead end. The

Athenians shut them in by barring the entrance with hoplites; then the *psiloi* who had followed the expedition stoned to death the Corinthian hoplites trapped inside.

In 426 the Athenian general Demosthenes invaded the mountains of Aetolia. The fate of his expeditionary force is described by Thucydides (3.97–8). He was short of *psiloi*, but did have a force of citizen archers in his army. As long as the arrows held out the Aetolians, who were not peltasts and so without shields for their own defence, were kept at bay. The archers were eventually routed, however, and the Athenian force broke up and fled. Many hid in a nearby forest, but the Aetolians set light to it and smoked them out. The Athenians lost 120 hoplites, men in the prime of life. Plate E is set in Aetolia in 426.

Plates E1, E2: Greek stone-thrower and javelinman

Greek *psiloi* are normally shown wearing the everyday dress of Greek shepherds: a tunic of coarse cloth and a shaggy felt hat. Sometimes there are modifications: one figure might wear a better tunic of linen, another might wear boots. One feature nearly all have in common is that they carry a makeshift shield formed by an animal pelt laid along the left arm and secured in place by knotting a pair of the paws around the neck. Weapons seem to be restricted to stones or javelins; only occasionally do we find the odd representation of a figure carrying a sword.

Plate E3: Athenian hoplite

A number of Athenian vases of the 430s, just on the eve of the Peloponnesian War, show Athenians carrying shields bearing the initials *A* or *ATHE*. Most vases of both these varieties show the figures engaged in the *hoplitodromos*—a foot race, run with helmet and shield, in which the ephebes took part. It is most probable that these shields were not used in war, but were used exclusively for these athletic contests. Though just possible, it is highly unlikely that such shields were ever issued by the state for campaign use, even to the young men. There does not seem to have been a uniform Athenian shield-design during this period. In fact we are told (Thuc. 4.96.3) that at Delium in 424 the Athenians—in surrounding the Thespians, who stood firm while

Greek *psilos* shown on an Attic amphora by The Providence Painter dating to the first half of the 5th century. He wears a tunic and shaggy felt hat, normal dress for Greek shepherds in antiquity, and protects himself with an animal skin. Note the absence of even a dagger for hand-to-hand combat. See Plate E1. (Musée du Louvre, G 216)

the rest of the Boeotian right flank fled—started to cut each other down, Athenian being unable to recognize Athenian in the confusion. In addition there are a couple of texts telling us the shield designs of individual generals: Nikias has a shield decorated with intricate workmanship in gold and purple (Plut. *Vit. Nic.* 28.5); and in the *Acharnians* (964–5, 1124, 1181) of Aristophanes the comic figure Lamachus uses a shield with the *gorgoneion* badge.

What relation the comic figure of Lamachus has to the *strategos* Lamachos of real life is unknown, but in the *Acharnians* Lamachus wears a triple-plumed helmet which included two white ostrich feathers (964–5, 1104, 1109). In the *Peace* (1172–74) a *taxiarch* is described as wearing a triple-crested helmet, and crimson clothing dyed with Sardian dye. In all probability, then, the triple-crested helmet was a badge of rank worn by both *taxiarch* and *strategos*.

Athenian Military Organisation

The tribal regiments had been commanded by ten *stratēgoi* during the Persian Wars. In the course of

This Attic *skyphos*, not far from the Battle of Kimolia in date, shows a peltast on one side and a stone-thrower on the other. Though crude, these paintings display some interesting features. Note the arrangement of the handles on the inside of the *peltē*, and the sword worn by the stone-thrower. (Vienna, Kunsthistorisches Museum, Inv. IV 1922)

time the majority of the *stratēgoi* started to become the equivalent of civilian ministers of war, and only one or two would take on the military responsibility of leading out an expedition. Each *taxis* was now commanded by a *taxiarch*, and was divided into a number of *lochoi*, each of a standard size, it seems, and commanded by a *lochagos*. The precise strength of the *taxis* would vary from expedition to expedition. For example, the Athenian people might pass a decree to send out an army of 5,000 hoplites. The *taxiarchs* would examine the muster rolls or *katalogoi*, on which the citizens liable for service were entered by archon-year. They would work out up to what archon-year the age-classes had to be called out to meet the number required. Such a levy was known as an 'eponymous levy'. An expedition involving a call-up for active service of all the age-classes up to the upper age limit was known as an expedition 'of the whole people' (*pandēmei*). On his fiftieth birthday a citizen passed from the active-service muster rolls to the reserve. Though occasionally the old men were called out for active-service, in general they were called upon to perform only garrison duty. Thucydides (2.13.6–8) gives the strength of the Athenian army on the outbreak of the Peloponnesian War as follows: 13,000 citizen hoplites of military age; 16,000 ephebes, old men and metics (foreign citizens permanently resident in Athens); 1,200 cavalry, including 200 horse-archers; 1,600 foot-archers; and 300 seaworthy triremes.

The Lakedaimonian Army at First Mantineia, 418 BC

After Herodotus' description of the army the Lakedaimonians sent to Plataea in 479, our next glimpse of their army comes in Thucydides' description of the battle of Mantineia (5.67–68). The organisational structure has changed somewhat, most probably as a result of the devastating earthquake of 464, which took so many Spartan lives, and the human losses suffered in the revolt of the Messenian helots that followed. The five *lochoi* were retained, though reduced in size, and further *lochoi* were created by emancipating helots 'of the most suitable type'. These newly enfranchised helots were known as *neodamodeis*.

At Mantineia there seem to have been five *lochoi* of citizens, each 512 strong and divided into four *pentekostyes* and 16 *enōmotiai*. The *enōmotia* of 32 men was drawn up eight deep with a frontage of four. This strength represented total Lakedaimonian citizen manpower up to the age of 55. We may assume that had the remaining age-classes been called up, the size of the *enōmotia* would have been

expanded accordingly. As with the Athenian system, call-up in the Lakedaimonian system was determined by age-class, and the summons might read, for example, that all were to report up to the 35th year of military liability. Squadding would then take place. So it seems that only 2,560 Spartans fought at Mantineia, which contrasts sharply with the 5,000 at Plataea. We are not told why the *perioikoi* were not called out for the battle.

In addition to the five citizen *lochoi* there were two more Lakedaimonian *lochoi* of *neodamodeis*, which seem to have numbered 1,000 men in total, and an eighth *lochos* of 600 Skiritai. The Skiritai were a community of Arcadians living on the borders of Lakedaimon, who seem to have enjoyed a 'most favoured *perioikoi*' status. They fought as hoplites at Mantineia. Of the two *lochoi* of *neodamodeis* one was known as the 'Brasideioi', because it was composed of helots who had been enfranchised after serving in a Thracian expedition under the Spartan general Brasidas.

Plate F1: Lakedaimonian hoplite, *c.* 413 BC

Around the middle of the 5th century the Lakedaimonians also started to lighten the equipment of their hoplites. Greaves and cuirass were discarded, and the closed Corinthian helmet was replaced by the open-faced 'Pilos-helmet'. Like the Boeotian helmet, the type seems to have originated in the Laconian variant of the felt *pilos* hat.

The two can be distinguished by the conical shape of the pilos-helmet, ending in quite a noticeable point, and by the shape of the rim. The pilos-helmet has a narrow rim which does not stick out at all, but which follows the line of the crown, hanging almost vertically from the body of the helmet. A feature of many Lakedaimonian pilos-helmets of this period is that the rim is slightly extended and rolled back a little above the neck.

Plate F1 is based on an Early Apulian vase-painting by 'The Painter of the Berlin Dancing Girl' dating to about 420 (A. D. Trendall & Alexander Cambitoglou, *The Red-Figured Vases of Apulia*, I, pl. 2, 5). We can identify the figure of the warrior as being a Lakedaimonian from his long hair and beard, which the Lakedaimonians were allowed to grow long on campaign, and which had fallen out of fashion everywhere else in the Greek world. The painter has obviously paid a lot of attention to detail, and it seems probable that the painting of the Lakedaimonian warrior is drawn from personal observation by the artist. The Lakedaimonian wears the characteristic pilos-helmet, and other interesting details shown are the spear head and butt. Of supreme interest is the layout of the inside of the shield. The bronze outer face of the shield was normally lined with thin layers of wood. This shield seems to have a bronze reinforcing band running round the inside where the rim meets the belly of the shield. This band secures a handle for the left hand (*antilabē*), and two shoulder straps which enabled the shield to be carried on the back when on the march. These two shoulder straps are shown in the painting as black curvy lines hanging loose on the inside of the shield. In the middle of the inside of the shield is placed a bronze arm-band (*porpax*) to which is attached the bronze arm-hole through which the left forearm is passed. Without the *porpax* the hoplite shield was useless, for it was this which held the shield securely to the arm. When the Lakedaimonian warrior returned home he took the *porpax* off his shield so that it could not be used by a helot in times of revolt.

The subject is shown naked, whereas we know that normally the Lakedaimonians wore crimson garments, especially a short-sleeved tunic, the *exōmis*, which was normally worn with the right shoulder unpinned and allowed to fall leaving the right arm and shoulder free for action. This

Ephebes (recruits) running in the armoured race. The marked shields would all be equal in weight: they were used in the armoured race to make sure no one was running with an artificially lightened shield. Small Attic *pelike* of around 430. (Laon, Municipal Museum of Archaeology, 371029)

the fallen Lakedaimonian warrior depicted on the Dexileos Monument. The idea behind the short sword seems to have been that it could be used for underarm thrusts, and was handier than the long-bladed sword in the close fighting of the phalanx. A short sword would be more liable to fall out of its sheath, however, which would have made the clips necessary. Soon the short-bladed sword spread to most other areas of Greece. Numerous reliefs of the period show this weapon in its sheath held in the left hand as well as the *antilabē*. This could have become a general practice either to prevent the sword falling out of its sheath, or to enable the sword to be located and drawn as quickly as possible in the case of the warrior's spear breaking during the mêlée.

Plate F2: Lakedaimonian officer, *c.* 413 BC

We have seen that there is considerable evidence that the equipment and dress of the Lakedaimonian army was remarkably uniform, and it is difficult to believe that by this stage the hoplite provided his own equipment rather than being provided with it by the state, as must certainly have been the case

garment is shown on numerous Attic grave reliefs of the period which show Lakedaimonian warriors defeated by the hand of the victorious Athenian— who may well have died himself in the process! The warrior on the Apulian vase, and the warriors on many of the Attic grave reliefs, are probably shown naked to emphasise the vulnerability of mortal flesh in combat, and probably at this stage do not represent actual military practice.

Numerous literary references refer to the small Lakedaimonian stabbing sword, and Attic reliefs showing Lakedaimonians often show a short sword, little more than a dagger, less than a foot long, and with a wide leaf- or diamond-shaped blade. No actual examples have survived, but a bronze simulacrum from Crete may have originally been attached to a statue honouring a Lakedaimonian king or general who fought on the island. F2 and F3 have been restored with swords based on these sources of information. The guard of the sword is hidden by the large mouth of the sheath. The edge of the mouth is not straight, but has raised semi-circular projections in the middle, which may have acted as clips to secure the sword in its sheath. These projections are clearly shown on the sheath used by

It is less certain that this vase shows an athletic scene because of the presence of the spear; other vases showing shields with the '*alpha*' device, however, show the armoured race. Also noteworthy is the bandeau worn underneath the helmet. This Nolan amphora by The Painter of the Boston Phiale dates to the 430s. Cf. Plate E3. (Warsaw, National Museum, 142338)

The scene on this Apulian calyx-crater probably reflects a genuine historical incident: the despatch of a Lakedaimonian expeditionary force to Italy in around 420. The Lakedaimonian's adversary, usually identified as an Amazon, is more probably a native cavalryman. Plate F1 is based on this figure, with his full beard and long hair so typically Lakedaimonian. (Wellesley, Mass., Wellesley College Museum)

with the emancipated helots. With the battle of Mantineia comes our first completely reliable piece of literary evidence for Lakedaimonian shield designs. A fragment of the poet Eupolis, which seems to come from a description of the array of forces at First Mantineia, tells us that the Lakedaimonians were distinguished by the letter *lambda* or 'L' for Lakedaimon on their shields, whereas the opposing Messenians bore the letter *mu* or 'M' for Messenia (Photius, *Onomasticon*, sv. 'Lambda'). How far back into the 5th century or earlier this practice went is unknown.

Plate F2 represents a Lakedaimonian officer. As has been mentioned above, it seems to have been common practice in Greek armies to differentiate rank by plumes or by other distinguishing marks on the helmet.

A Lakedaimonian shield was discovered in a cistern during excavations in the Athenian Agora in 1936. This shield had been captured in 425 when the Lakedaimonian garrison at Sphakteria, 420 men plus helots, had surrendered. The Lakedaimonians had been outmanoeuvred and penned up on the island, which lay just offshore of Pylos, where an Athenian expeditionary force had made a landing in Messenia. The Athenian general Demosthenes, who had learned well from his earlier defeat in Aetolia, landed on the island following a destructive forest fire. The Lakedaimonians were then worn down by incessant missile fire from Demosthenes' light-armed troops, and were eventually forced to surrender. The fortuitous discovery of this shield allows us to restore the cable pattern of the shield rim of plate F2 with some accuracy.

Plate F3: Tegean hoplite, *c.* 413 BC

The Tegeans were the most faithful allies of the Lakedaimonians and held the most honourable position in the battle line after them. At Plataea there were 1,500 Tegean hoplites, plus an equal number of *psiloi* to accompany them. At the battle of Nemea in 394 there may have been as many as 2,400. Plate F3 is based on the tombstone of Lisas the Tegean.

His dress and equipment are obviously modelled

Grave relief of Stratokles son of Prokles. Dating from around the turn of the 5th century, this relief shows the Athenian Stratokles triumphant over a fallen warrior, who is probably a Peloponnesian and possibly a Lakedaimonian. The latter wears an *exōmis* pinned up at the shoulder. Note also his short sword and pilos-helmet. (Boston, Museum of Fine Arts, nr.64)

army consisted of Lakedaimonian helots, allies and mercenaries, and it is highly probable that all these units were composed of hoplites dressed in exactly the same dress: pilos-helmet, crimson tunic etc., differentiated one from another only by the design painted on to the bronze shield.

The colours of the Tegean's clothing and equipment have been restored bearing these factors in mind. His shield design may have simply been the letter *tau*, 'T' for Tegea, which we see on contemporary coinage of the city. We also know that the Sicyonians bore the letter *sigma* painted on their shields from an anecdote in Xenophon (*Hell.* 4.4.10). This tells how Pasimachus, a Lakedaimonian cavalry officer, the Sicyonian infantry having fled, dismounted his men and took up the shields of the Sicyonians. He then advanced against the enemy saying 'By Castor and Pollux, Argives, these *sigmas* will deceive you!' They certainly did—for the Argives, thinking their adversaries were only Sicyonians, slew the lot of them.

The Mantineian Army

Mantineia, lying close to Tegea, was the most powerful Arcadian community. The two states were locked in an almost continuous struggle for hegemony in the region. Tegea tended to look to Lakedaimon for support, whereas the more distant Mantineia used to look towards Lakedaimon's traditional enemies such as the Argives. This explains why Tegea stuck so long to her traditional Lakedaimonian alignment.

Fortunately we know rather more about the Mantineian army than we do about the Tegean. The Mantineian citizenry were divided into five demes, and the army was correspondingly divided into five regiments called Epalea, Enyalia, Hoplodmia, Posoidaia, and Wanakisia (*IG* 5.2.271). The army consisted of about 3,000 hoplites in all, so each of the regiments probably numbered about 600.

The shield device of the Mantineian hoplite was the trident of Poseidon, the patron deity of the city of Mantineia. This must have been adopted as the standard shield device quite early on, for Bacchylides, who flourished around the middle of the 5th century, mentions it (frg.[Bergk]41) in one of his poems.

very closely on Lakedaimonian lines, as we can see from the shape of the shield's arm-hole, the tunic and especially the pilos-helmet: these were perhaps general for all Lakedaimon's Peloponnesian allies. A number of texts indicate the uniformity of dress in armies under Lakedaimonian influence. The army of Greek mercenaries serving under Cyrus the Younger was commanded by the Spartan Clearchus, 'with spear in one hand and staff in the other', and was largely trained and organised by him along Lakedaimonian lines. Xenophon (*Anab.* 1.2.16) describes the army drawn up for parade in crimson tunics and bronze helmets and greaves. Some time after this Xenophon (*Ages.* 2.7) tells us that the army Agesilaus took back to the Greek mainland from Asia on the outbreak of the Corinthian War was dressed entirely in crimson and bronze. This

The Lakedaimonian Hegemony

Bronze model of a short sword from Crete. It is 32.3cm long, perhaps slightly larger than life-size, and weighs 780 grams. The serrated edge to the blade is difficult to explain. The use of short swords such as these spread throughout Greek armies under Lakedaimonian influence. (British Museum, 1931.2–17.2)

The defeat of Athens in the Peloponnesian War left Lakedaimon as the most powerful state in all Greece. In order to achieve this victory, however, the Lakedaimonians had had to alter their traditional way of doing things to such an extent that the spirit of the Lycurgan constitution was seriously undermined. In order to build and maintain a fleet the Lakedaimonians had had to accept Persian subsidies, and these large amounts of money passing through Lakedaimonian hands soon made their corrupting influence felt. The new empire also required Spartan governors or generals to live for long periods of time away from Sparta. Once away from the imposed restraints of the Lycurgan system these Spartans went wild, and their debauched and venal behaviour soon made the Spartans detested in many of the states where they had previously been so admired. Few Spartans wanted to return to the cold comforts of Sparta after a lengthy sojourn in foreign fleshpots.

The decline of Lakedaimonian integrity could have been avoided had the state not decided on a policy of imperialism following the end of the Peloponnesian War. This policy was foisted on the Lakedaimonian state by the general Lysander and the lame King Agesilaus. The Lakedaimonians became embroiled in a war with Persia over the suzerainty of the Greek cities of Asia. Meanwhile, growing hostility to Lakedaimon finally erupted in 395 in the form of the Corinthian War, with most of the states of central Greece combined in an alliance against Lakedaimon. The Lakedaimonians acted quickly, and an allied force under Lysander was sent into Boeotia. The two armies met at Haliartos, and in the ensuing battle Lysander was killed.

The Army of the Boeotian League

We are fortunate in having some information concerning the organisation of the Boeotian League at the beginning of the 4th century. Much important information has been preserved in a fragment of papyrus found at the site of the ancient Ptolemaic town of Oxyrhynchus, and known as the *Hellenica Oxyrhynchia* in consequence. This passage describes the state of the Boeotian League in 395. Boeotia was divided into 11 sections, each one of which supplied a federal magistrate known as a Boeotarch and a military contingent of 1,000 hoplites and 100 cavalry in time of war. The Thebans supplied four Boeotarchs, two representing Thebes itself and two more who had originally represented Plataea, Skolos, Erythrai, Skaphai and other places now conquered by Thebes. Orchomenos and Hysiai supplied a further two, as did Thespiai Eutresis and Thisbai. Tanagra supplied one. Haliartos Lebadeia and Koroneia supplied one in turn, as did Akraiphion Kopia and Chaironeia.

Plates G1, G2: Boeotian hoplites, *c.* 395 BC

These two figures are based on Boeotian painted pots which have been dated to the last decade of the 5th and the first decade of the 4th centuries (Reinhard Lullies, *Ath. Mitt.* 65, 1940, pp. 1–27). Both the Boeotian painted pottery and the Boeotian incised grave reliefs of this period display many interesting features of dress and equipment which may well be characteristically Boeotian. One distinctive feature seems to be the highly decorated shield interiors. Figures of heroes or minor deities seem to be especially popular. The interior of plate

Bronze statuette from Sparta. The figure, probably taking part in a religious festival at home in Sparta, which would explain the shaved chin and the nudity, would once have carried a spear and a shield which have now become detached from the figure. The peculiarly shaped plume is probably a badge of rank, and is used in the reconstruction of Plate F2. (Sparta, The Archaeological Museum, 970)

G1's shield is decorated with a Triton. Paradoxically, the Boeotian helmet is hardly ever seen: the pilos-helmet predominates, and most other types are encountered. Greek helmets do not seem to have been given a padded lining for the comfort of the wearer. The warrior would either wear a close-fitting cap known as a *kataityx*, or would wrap a bandeau round his head—as has plate G2—to ensure his comfort.

The clothing worn by these figures is minimal—perhaps only a wrap and frequently nothing at all; and one wonders if, bearing in mind the ubiquity of the nude in military art in the early years of the 4th century, Greek warriors in fact fought naked during these years. In Boeotia this may have been exceptionally popular, for, as well as their other strange habits, the Boeotians almost worshipped the body, spending most of their lives in the gymnasia. There is no information on the colours of the garments worn, though the incised grave reliefs did preserve some red. One unusual feature noticeable in many representations of Boeotian hoplites (as with plate G2) is that they wear boots. Elsewhere in Greece hoplites invariably fought bare-footed.

Many of the painted pots bear a snake as a shield device. Pausanias (8.11.8) tells us that the tomb of Epameinondas at Mantineia was decorated with a shield with a snake upon it, intended to signify that he was a member of the clan of the Spartioi. Plutarch (*Vit. Lys.* 29.6) tells us that Lysander, although it had been prophesied that he would die from snake-bite, was killed in battle by one Neochoros of Haliartus, who bore the device of a serpent (or dragon, for in Ancient Greece the two were the same) on his shield. It may be that Neochoros, too, was one of the Spartioi.

Plate G3: Theban hoplite, *c.* 395 BC

State shield devices do not seem to have been used in Boeotia during this period, for there is no tie-up between the shield devices shown on Boeotian representations of hoplites and the known badges of the cities of Boeotia. The only possible exception is Thebes, whose emblem we know to have been the club of Herakles, the patron deity. Representations of hoplites with clubs are sufficiently rare in Greek art to make us think that the club was not a common shield device, so where they do occur it may be that the artist wishes to show a Theban.

Drawings of the Lakedaimonian shield found in the Agora, and of the cable-design of the rim. The punched inscription tells us that the Athenians took the shield from the Lakedaimonians at Pylos. In its present state the shield is slightly oval, measuring 95 by 83cm. Cf. Plate F2. (American School of Classical Studies at Athens: Agora Excavations)

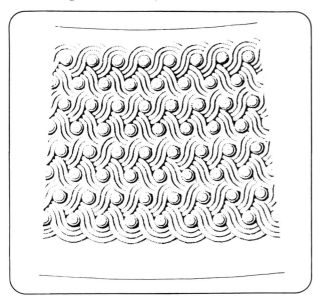

Plate G3 is based on a Lucanian vase (A. D. Trendall, *The Red-Figured Vases of Lucania, Campania and Sicily*, Oxford, 1967, p. 44, nr. 216) now in the British Museum (F 177).

In 387/6 the Peace of Antalkidas, which brought the Corinthian War to an end, broke up the Boeotian League; and in 383 the citadel of Thebes, the Kadmeia, was siezed by the Spartan Phoebidas in a surprise raid. Thereafter a Lakedaimonian garrison was permanently installed in the Kadmeia. The Lakedaimonians were only expelled from the Kadmeia by a band of Theban patriots, which included Epameinondas and Pelopidas, in 379. Interestingly enough the coins of Boeotia dating to the period 387 to 379, while still retaining the device of the Boeotian shield which was traditionally shown on coinage of the League, now show the badge of the individual city on top of the Boeotian shield. These badges seem to belong to the patron deities of the cities concerned.

Organisation of the Lakedaimonian army, *c.* 413–*c.* 371 BC

In 403 a new organisation is mentioned in the Lakedaimonian army, the *mora* or 'division' (Xen. *Hell.* 2.4.31). The idea behind the *mora*, with its integral unit of cavalry, seems to have been to divide the army up into self-sufficient divisions which could operate independently of the main army. This would have become necessary when the Lakedaimonians were increasingly forced to maintain permanent garrisons on foreign soil. It was impossible to task the whole field army with this duty on a permanent basis; so a portion of the army,

Restorations of Peloponnesian shield designs, according to the shapes of badges or letters on contemporary or near-contemporary coinage. Shield blazons of Mantineia, Messenia, Sicyon and a conjectural one for Tegea are shown. (Drawing: Hugh Coddington)

A detailed account of the organisation of the *mora* is given in chapter 11 of Xenophon's pamphlet entitled *The Constitution of the Lakedaimonians*. Each of the six *morai* in the army was commanded by a *polemarch*, and was divided into four *lochoi* each commanded by a *lochagos*, eight *pentekostyes* each commanded by a *pentekontēres*, and sixteen *enōmotiai* each commanded by an *enōmotarch*. The *enōmotia* was now, it seems, raised in strength to 36 men, who could be drawn up in three files of 12—as was the case at Leuctra—or six files of six. This gave the *mora* a total notional strength of 592 hoplites and the army a strength of 3,552.

The *mora* also had its own integral *mora* of cavalry attached. The Lakedaimonians had first raised a body of cavalry, together with a force of archers, in 424 when the Athenians occupied Pylos and Kythera (Thuc. 4.55.2). Presumably these troops were not distributed among the *lochoi*. When the *lochoi* were replaced by the six *morai*, however, the cavalry was expanded to 600 and divided up into six *morai*, each commanded by a *hipparmost*. During pitched battles the cavalry was drawn up together on the wings; but on campaign, if the *morai* were operating independently, each *mora* was given its own cavalry *mora* to help drive off peltast attacks. The *mora* of horse was divided into two *oulamoi* of 50 men each, which would be stationed one either side of the hoplites. The *oulamos* seems to have been divided into ten files of five, each called a *pempas* under a *pempadarch*, and drawn up in a square.

Given the fact that the hoplite force alone, as well as the combined force of hoplites and horse, were both called *mora*, it is hardly surprising that there should be some confusion in the ancient sources as to what the precise strength of the *mora* was. Plutarch (*Vit. Pel.* 17.2) tells us that Ephorus says the *mora* numbered 500; Callisthenes, 700; and Polybius, 900. Though the *morai* were disbanded following the battle of Leuctra in 371, they were probably re-introduced in Hellenistic times when the citizen body of Sparta was massively expanded during a period of revolutionary reform. It is probably these *morai* to which Polybius refers. All

The funerary *stele* of Lisas the Tegean, on which Plate F3 is based, was found during terracing work undertaken on royal estates near the village of Tatoi around 1874. It seems to have come from the necropolis of the nearby Peloponnesian fortress of Dekeleia. Originally the spear and other details would have been painted in. (After *BCH* 4, 1880, p. 408–15. pl. VII)

usually two *morai*, would perform such garrison duties in rotation. The first of these permanent garrisons to be established by the Lakedaimonians was that at Dekeleia in Attica in 413, so perhaps the reorganisation of the army from *lochoi* to *morai* took place in 413 or shortly thereafter. Because of the long absences from home it would not have been desirable to have the *morai* organised along any regional or tribal lines, so it is reasonable to suppose that the obal system of recruitment was abandoned too.

Boeotian grave relief of Rhynchon, now in Thebes Archaeological Museum (55), and probably dating to 424. Note the highly decorated inside surface of the shield, and the boots, both distinctive Boeotian features. Note also the sword held in the left hand, ready for instant use. Cf. Plate G. (After Ernst Pfuhl, *Malerei und Zeichnung der Griechen*, 1923, pl. 634)

the other figures—500, 600 and 700—can be reconciled with a *mora* of slightly less than 600 hoplites, rounded up or down, together with or excluding a *mora* of 100 cavalry. These figures, of course, give only the notional state of the *mora*, and it is possible that on campaign several *morai* would find themselves below strength. They also give the normal full fighting strength of the *mora* with the first 35 age-classes called up, that is from ages 20 to 55. In times of national emergency we might find the first 40 age-classes called out, as happened after Leuctra. Normally those holding office were also exempted from military service, but after Leuctra these too were called up.

It seems fairly certain that by now the *morai* were manned by Spartiates, *perioikoi*, and *neodamodeis* all fighting side by side. Four *morai* with a total strength of 2,768 men fought at Leuctra, but we are told that only 700 Spartiates took part in the battle. Of these 300 would have formed the Royal Guard, so in this battle only a seventh of the line troops were Spartiates.

Plate H1: Lakedaimonian cavalryman, *c.* 382 BC

The representational evidence unearthed by archaeological excavations at Sparta is as yet small, and it should not surprise us that nothing we can identify as a Lakedaimonian cavalryman has yet been found. On the other hand, a large number of representations of the Lakedaimonian heroes Castor and Pollux have been found. These show the two horsemen quite uniformly equipped, and it may be that their dress copies that normally worn by the Lakedaimonian cavalry. The monuments invariably show the divine twins wearing a *pilos*-shaped hat or helmet. A medium-length sword is also usually shown, as well as a cavalry spear. Sometimes a cloak may be shown, and occasionally a tunic as well. This evidence has been carefully gathered together and used for the reconstruction of Plate H1.

Plate H2: Macedonian hoplite, *c.* 382 BC

In 382 the Lakedaimonians sent an allied army to help King Amyntas of Macedonia win back his lands from the Olynthians. Macedonia was mostly famed for its cavalry, and in early times its infantry seems to have been little more than a poorly

Lullies attributed this Boetian cantharos, on which plate G1 is based, to The Painter of the Great Athens Cantharos. What the iconographic significance of the bird and the wreath might be is unknown. Note the highly-decorated inside of the shield. (Athens, National Museum, 12486)

equipped band of peasants. Some time around the end of the 5th century, however, or in the early 4th, one of the Macedonian kings raised a force of hoplites. Unfortunately, we do not know which king it was. A number of tantalising passages have survived describing military reform; for example, Thucydides (2.100.2) tells us that Archelaus (413–399) built fortresses, cut roads, and organised the cavalry for war by providing horses, arms, and other equipment. Little is said in any of these passages, however, about the hoplites. Neither do we know whether the titles of infantry regiments which we find in later Macedonian armies, such as hypaspists or *pezhetairoi*, were first awarded to infantry regiments in these early times, or whether they date back no further than the age of Philip and Alexander.[1]

Plate H2 is based on a funerary relief of the period found at Pella. The equipment is similar to that worn by the Lakedaimonians and all their allies; even so, it is surprising to see Lakedaimonian

[1]See MAA 148, *The Army of Alexander the Great*

1: Lakedaimonian officer, c.490 BC
2: Samian hoplite, c.490 BC
3: Argive hoplite, early 5th C.
4: Athenian hoplite of Alkmaionid Clan, c.490 BC

1   2   4   3

A

B

1: Thracian peltast, 440s BC
2, 3: Greek ekdromoi, 440s BC

1: Boeotian hoplite, c.440 BC
2, 3: Thessalian cavalrymen, c.440 BC

C

1: Athenian cavalryman, c.440 BC
2: Athenian cavalry recruit, c.430 BC

D

1, 2: Greek psiloi, c.426 BC
3: Athenian hoplite, c.426 BC

E

1: Lakedaimonian hoplite, c.413 BC
2: Lakedaimonian officer, c.413 BC
3: Tegean hoplite, c.413 BC

F

1, 2: Boeotian hoplites, c.395 BC
3: Theban hoplite, c.395 BC

Angus McBride

G

H

1: Lakedaimonian cavalryman, c.382 BC
2: Macedonian hoplite, c.382 BC
3: Cretan mercenary archer

1: Arcadian picked hoplite, 364 BC
2: Eleian picked hoplite, 364 BC

I

1: Thessalian javelinman, c.362 BC
2: Aenianian javelinman, c.362 BC
3: Theban general officer

J

3

1: Athenian hamippos, c.349 BC
2: Athenian prodromos cavalryman, c.349 BC
3: Euboean hoplite, c.349 BC

K

1: Athenian hoplite, second half 4th C. BC
2: Rhodian hoplite, end of 4th C. BC
3: Greek mercenary, c.330s BC
4: Baggage-carrier

L

influence spreading so far north. The figure on the relief wears only a thin wrap-around cloak or *ephaptis*, and we have no way of knowing if this is due to 'heroic nudity' or if the Macedonian hoplites did, in fact, fight almost naked. The shield is based on a painting of a shield found on the wall of a Macedonian chamber tomb dating to the reign of Amyntas III (393–369). The tomb has been fully published by K. Despinis in the Greek archaeological journal *Archaiologika Analekta ex Athenon* 13, 1980, pp. 198–209. This shield design, together with the others found painted on the walls of the tomb, may simply be the device used by an individual and may have no further significance than that.

Plate H3: Cretan mercenary archer

Units of Cretan mercenary archers serving with the Lakedaimonians are attested in a number of surviving passages, though none mention their presence during the campaign in the Chakidikē.

Representations of Cretan archers are exceedingly rare, and none come from the Classical period. We have reconstructed plate H3, therefore, on the hypothesis that if we show a figure in Cretan regional dress with the addition of a few necessary military items, we shall not be far off the mark. The basis for our reconstruction is a Hellenistic grave relief which shows many features of Cretan dress. Perhaps the most interesting is the head-band or turban, which is shown on a few more ancient representations of Cretans, and which has formed part of Cretan traditional costume right up to the present day. There is no evidence whatever as to what colour these Cretans may have dressed in, so we have taken the opportunity to show plate H3 dressed in black, the preferred colour of Cretan traditional dress in modern times. Boots also seem to have been worn frequently in ancient times, just as they are in modern Crete; but unfortunately the relief is broken just above where the boots would (or would not) have been shown, so it is perhaps wisest to leave them out!

What distinguished the Cretan archer from his Greek counterpart was the small bronze *peltē* the Cretan carried. In the *Anabasis* (5.2.28–32) Xenophon describes how some Cretan archers set a false ambush when the Greek army was being pursued by native warriors along the road towards Trapezos. The Cretans hid in the undergrowth

This Boeotian cantharos shows, on the left, a seated figure wearing a Boeotian hat. On the right stands a hoplite, naked but for his boots, with a spear and shield. He has removed his helmet: note the bandeau. Plate G2 is based on this hoplite. (Athens, National Museum, 1373)

covering a hill above the road, but allowed their bronze *peltai* to gleam through the branches. This made the enemy think they were about to be ambushed, so they ceased chasing the main army and went after the ambushers. We have no information as to what shield-designs the Cretans may have painted on their shields. Coins of Polyrhenia, probably Hellenistic in date, show shields decorated with a bull's head.

Cretan archery equipment was also a little different from that used elsewhere in Greece. The quiver was fitted with a flap which could be drawn over the mouth. The arrowheads were large and heavy, cast in bronze, and of a distinctive shape. In later periods the arrow shaft would be made from reed and the flights would be made from a vulture's wing feather: the same materials were probably used in antiquity. The purpose of the bag hung around the neck is unknown, but it may have been used to carry spare archery equipment, such as bowstrings, which could be damaged by rain.

The Expansion of Thebes

Lakedaimon's power was smashed forever at the battle of Leuctra in 371. Her losses in manpower were heavy; her loss in prestige was catastrophic. The Theban victory was followed by a number of invasions of the Peloponnese, and Lakedaimonian power over the peninsula came to an end. The small states of the Peloponnese now banded together in federal leagues to guarantee their independence.

Probably the most powerful and the most successful of these was the Arcadian League, which was mainly the creation of one Lykomedes of Mantineia. The League was established in 370, and provisions were soon made to establish a standing army to guarantee its independence. Arcadians had been the most numerous of Greek mercenaries to seek service abroad for many years, so there was no shortage of available manpower, only of money to pay them. A force of 5,000 picked troops was established, called the *Eparitoi*, which seems to have had the same meaning as *epilektoi* in the Arcadian dialect.

It was inevitable that these newly independent states would soon start to clash with each other. Disputes were won by treachery and subterfuge more often than by battles and sieges. Aeneas of Stymphalus, who as general of the Arcadian League in 367 was responsible for driving the tyrant Euphron out of Sicyon, formulated his experiences learned during these times in the manual we know as the *Polyorkētika* or 'Siege Operations' of Aeneas Tacticus (transl. Loeb), which was published in 357/6. It was not long before the Arcadian League, ever expanding by the adhesion of more and more Arcadian communities, clashed with Elis over the possession of some Arcadian towns on the Eleian border. The Arcadians formed an alliance with the Pisatans, a small community lying to the south of Elis who had long disputed the stewardship of the Olympic Games with the Eleians.

Plate I: The Olympic Games of 364 BC

In 364 the Arcadians marched against Olympia and celebrated the 104th Olympiad, while troops of the Achaean League marched to help the Eleians. The Eleians resisted the Arcadian invasion with all their forces, and a fierce battle took place actually on the games ground, in front of the crowd. The combatants had as spectators the Greeks who were present for the Games; wearing festive wreaths on

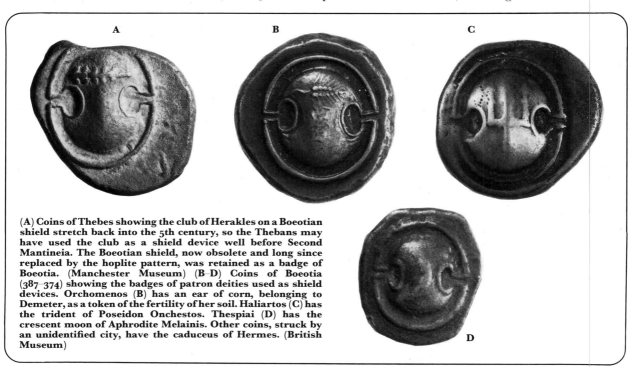

(A) Coins of Thebes showing the club of Herakles on a Boeotian shield stretch back into the 5th century, so the Thebans may have used the club as a shield device well before Second Mantineia. The Boeotian shield, now obsolete and long since replaced by the hoplite pattern, was retained as a badge of Boeotia. (Manchester Museum) (B–D) Coins of Boeotia (387–374) showing the badges of patron deities used as shield devices. Orchomenos (B) has an ear of corn, belonging to Demeter, as a token of the fertility of her soil. Haliartos (C) has the trident of Poseidon Onchestos. Thespiai (D) has the crescent moon of Aphrodite Melainis. Other coins, struck by an unidentified city, have the caduceus of Hermes. (British Museum)

their heads, they calmly applauded the outstanding deeds of valour on both sides, themselves out of reach of danger. The Arcadians had already held the horse race and the pentathlon. As the Eleians, fighting with unaccustomed bravery, pushed them out of the race-course, the wrestling events had to take place between the race-course and the altar. The Eleians had by this time reached the sacred precinct. Here they came upon a line of Arcadian hoplites, and scattered them; a running fight developed in the sacred complex, where the Arcadians took to the roofs and pelted the Eleians below with tiles. It was here that the Eleian general Stratolas, the leader of the 'Three Hundred', was killed, and the Eleians retired. Over the next night the Arcadians and their allies dismantled the merchants' booths around the sacred precinct and built a stockade from them. When the Eleians arrived the next day and saw the stockade, they abandoned their attempt to regain the stewardship of the Games, retired, and declared the year 364 'Anolympiad'.

Plate I1: Arcadian picked hoplite, 364 BC

Evidence as to the dress of the troops of the various Leagues is, unfortunately, very scarce, so the figures in this plate are largely hypothetical. There are a few clues, however, which suggest that these reconstructions are at least along the right lines. This figure wears a 'Phrygian' helmet and a muscle-cuirass. It seems that Greek hoplites started to re-equip themselves with heavy body armour during the 360s. In *The Army of Alexander the Great* (MAA 148) I suggested that the change might have come about under Macedonian influence after the battle of Chaironeia in 338. In fact Athenian reliefs which can now be dated to the 360s already show the new style of armour; so it was adopted by Philip under Greek influence, not the other way round. Though the 'Phrygian' helmet is shown in Lycian reliefs which may date back to the 380s, the first appearance of this style of helmet in Greek art other than Attic which can be given a firm date is on a stater of the Achaean League dating to the 360s. Presumably this helmet represents a type worn by troops of the League, though it is possible that it represents a trophy captured from Achaea's enemies.

The bronze hoplite shield of Plate I1 is painted

This relief was dedicated to Castor and Pollux by Menandros, the Lakedaimonian harmost (governor) of Kythera. The letter-forms seem to date the relief to the 3rd century, but the style of dress probably goes back to the 4th. Though badly worn, this relief shows details of the tunic and cloak not preserved elsewhere, which have been used to reconstruct Plate H1. (Athens, National Museum, 1437)

with a ligature of the two initial letters of Arcadia, '*alpha*' and '*rho*'. This design appears on contemporary coins of the Arcadian League, and it would have been the natural choice as a shield design for the *Eparitoi*.

Plate I2: Eleian picked hoplite, 364 BC

Xenophon mentions two bands of Eleian *epilektoi*, the 'Three Hundred' and the 'Four Hundred'. We are poorly informed on Eleian internal politics at this time, but Xenophon (*Hell.* 7.4.13 & 31) tells us that Stratolas, one of the leaders of the oligarchic party in Elis, was also leader of the 'Three Hundred'. The clash between the oligarchic and democratic parties in Elis came in 365. The Arcadians gave support to the democratic party, and Charopos siezed the Eleian acropolis. The cavalry and the 'Three Hundred' ejected the garrison from the acropolis, however, and 'about

Four Hundred citizens' including Argeios and Charopos were banished. It seems reasonable to suppose that the 'Three Hundred' were a body of troops retained by the oligarchic party, while the 'Four Hundred' were a corresponding force maintained by the democrats.

Interestingly enough, Elis started to mint two

Funerary relief from Pella, used in the reconstruction of Plate H2. The Macedonian capital was only moved from Aigai to Pella around 400, so it is unlikely that this relief is any earlier in date. The pilos-helmet is probably worn as a result of Lakedaimonian influence. (Istanbul, Archaeological Museum, 85)

new series of coins about 370. One shows an eagle, the bird of Olympian Zeus, tearing a hare, all on a hoplite shield. The other shows an eagle attacking a snake—again on a hoplite shield. The eagle of Zeus is the normal badge which appears on most Eleian coinage, but the shield indicates that the same badge was used as a shield device by Eleian troops during the 360s. It may well be that these coins were struck to pay the 'Three Hundred' and the 'Four Hundred', the two types of shield designs on the coins representing the shield devices of the two units. Unfortunately, we have no idea which unit might have used which device.

At the feet of the two principal figures of plate I is shown a fallen hoplite of the Achaean League. His bronze shield is painted with a ligature of the letters 'alpha' and 'chi', the two initial letters of Achaea, which frequently appears as a badge on coins of the League.

The Mantineian Campaign

From 364 onwards the Arcadians decided to maintain the *Eparitoi* by using the sacred treasures of Olympia. This decision eventually caused the dissolution of the League. The Mantineians and the Tegeans, traditionally at loggerheads over the control of south-eastern Arcadia, soon fell out: the pretext was the misuse of the temple funds. A vote was passed in the Assembly of the League not to use the temple treasures, and the *Eparitoi* were no longer paid. Those who could not serve in the *Eparitoi* without pay quickly melted away, while those who could encouraged their rich friends to enroll in order that they should gain political power over the democratic League. In these circumstances, with the League in danger of breaking up or being taken over by the oligarchic faction, the Tegeans together with most of the Arcadians appealed to the Thebans to intervene in the Peloponnese once more, while the Mantineians and some others of the Arcadians appealed to the Spartans for help.

Plate J: The Battle of Mantineia, 362 BC

Epameinondas, the Theban general, invaded the Peloponnese with a huge army of Thebans together with their allies—Euboeans, Locrians, Sicyonians, Malians, Aenianians, Thessalians and others; and in the Peloponnese they were joined by the Tegeans, together with most of the Arcadians, the Argives, the Messenians and other Peloponnesian allies. He was opposed by an army of Mantineians with a few other Arcadians, Lakedaimonians, Eleians, Athenians, and others. The Achaean League seems to have been split in just the same way as the Arcadian, for Achaean troops fought on both sides.

Epameinondas made a lightning raid on Sparta, but, having failed to capture that city, he doubled back and marched rapidly on Mantineia. Again, as ill luck would have it, he failed to capture that city despite all his brilliant manoeuvres. He now resolved to offer battle before quitting the Peloponnese. This decision was probably influenced by the fact that of the 12 Lakedaimonian *lochoi* into which the army had been reorganised after Leuctra, only three were present. How these new *lochoi* were organised and what strength they stood at is entirely unknown. It is fairly safe to assume, however, that the Lakedaimonians no longer had the resources of manpower available to man *lochoi* of the same strength as the old 12 *lochoi* of the abandoned *morai*. All the Lakedaimonian horsemen were present at the battle, however, together with their mercenary peltasts and the Cretan archers. At Mantineia the Lakedaimonian cavalry were drawn up six deep (Xen. *Hell.* 7.5.23), so it seems that the old organisation of the *oulamos* and *pempas* had been abandoned too.

The battle was fought in the dusty Mantineian Plain in the height of summer. Epameinondas concentrated his forces on the left and delivered the enemy right flank a shattering charge. In the course of the fighting, however, Epameinondas received a mortal spear-wound in the chest. So ended the battle which everyone had expected to decide the fate of Greece for the next generation. There was even more confusion and disorder in Greece after it than there had been before.

The Thessalian League

Thessaly was again united by Jason, Tyrant of Pherai, who was elected *tagos* of the League in 374. Jason replaced the obsolete *klēros* with the city-state as the territorial basis on which the forces of the League were levied. The forces of the League now numbered 8,000 horse and 20,000 hoplites plus a huge number of peltasts. The perioikic communities continued to pay the same level of tribute as had been fixed in the time of Skopas. Jason also

Πυρρίας : Πυρρία
Ὑπερβάλλωνος : Μενεκάρτην.

Hellenistic grave relief from Kakodiki in the White Mountains of Crete. The relief is now lost, but fortunately a drawing was made of it while it was lodged in the taverna of Spyridon Kalaitskakis in Chania. Representations of Cretan archers are most rare. This one is particularly good, as it shows details of regional dress such as the turban, worn up to the present day in Crete. See Plate H3 for a reconstruction. (After M. Guarducci, *Inscriptiones Creticae* II, vi, 7, p. 88)

introduced purely military reforms into the Thessalian army. For example, it was he who invented the rhomboid formation, from which the wedge, utilized so successfully by Alexander of Macedon, was derived. There is little doubt that Jason would have gone on to impose his power on the whole of Greece, as Philip of Macedon was to do later on, but Jason was assassinated before his plans came to fruition. Jason was eventually succeeded as Tyrant of Pherai by one Alexander, but Alexander could never attain the *tageia*, which lapsed. At the time of Mantineia the dominions of Alexander of Pherai and the lands of the Thessalian League were quite separate. Both were in alliance with Thebes, and both sent separate contingents which fought at Mantineia.

Shielded archers are depicted but rarely in Greek art. This *dinos*, or mixing-bowl, by The Altamura Painter, may perhaps be taken to indicate the presence of Cretans in Athens around 450. Other figures on the bowl wear the Thracian helmet, which is typical for the period. (University of Newcastle Upon Tyne, Greek Museum, 52)

Plate J1: Thessalian javelinman, c. 362 BC

The Thebans had in their army a great number of slingers and javelinmen from Thessaly and from the Thessalian perioikis. The perioikic hill folk, from the mountainous areas which surrounded the Thessalian Plain—Magnesia, Perrhaebia and elsewhere—were accustomed to using these weapons from boyhood. At the battle of Mantineia the Thessalian *psiloi* played a major part in the defeat of the Athenian cavalry on the left flank. This figure is based on a contemporary coin of Pelinna in Thessalia Hestiaiotis.

Plate J2: Aenianian javelinman, c. 362 BC

The Aenianes were another tributary people of the Thessalians who supplied the League's army with skirmish troops. This figure is based on a contemporary coin of the Aenianes. Both J1 and J2 are using javelin thongs. The thong would be fixed on to the javelin with a temporary hitch knot, and form a loop which was hooked round the index finger; it fell off the javelin when it was thrown, and was retained in the hand. The colours restored to both figures J1 and J2 are arbitrary.

Plate J3: Theban general officer

Xenophon (*Hell.* 7.5.20) tells us that at Mantineia the cavalry whitened their helmets, and the Arcadian hoplites painted clubs on their shields in imitation of the Thebans. It is reasonable to assume that by this period the Boeotian helmet was in use both among the Theban infantry and the cavalry. The cavalry probably painted their helmets white as a field sign. The Boeotian helmet was almost certainly in use among other cavalry forces present at Mantineia, including the Athenians, and the white paint avoided confusion in the heat of battle. The Theban badge of the club was possibly painted on the shields of all the Boeotian contingents. Since the liberation of Thebes in 379 the Thebans had increased their domination of the League, eliminating hostile cities like Orchomenos, until the Boeotian League had virtually become a synonym for the city of Thebes. It is very difficult to assess how much political independence the other remaining cities of Boeotia retained, but the answer is probably very little.

The Arcadians who painted clubs on their shields would be the Tegeans and the bulk of the Arcadians who had invited the Thebans into the Peloponnese. Whether the Mantineians and the other Arcadians still used the 'AR' badge of the Arcadians on their shields, or individual city badges such as the trident of Mantineia, is unknown.

Plate J3 has been swathed in a crimson general's cloak. It is a great pity we have no representational evidence for Theban infantry dress during the 360s, for this might enable us to discover what part the Thebans played in the re-adoption of body armour during this period. It may be that the Thebans played a crucial rôle, and that the armouring of infantry was connected with the new tactics developed by Epameinondas. Given the present state of our knowledge, however, this is pure speculation.

The Theban Army

The Theban hoplites were organised into *lochoi* of 300 (eg. Xen. *Hell.* 7.4.36) each commanded by a *lochagos*. The Thebans preferred to draw up their *lochoi* in deep formations to deliver an irresistible blow against the enemy line. At Delion in 424 the *lochoi* were drawn up in 12 files each 25 men deep; at Leuctra they were drawn up in six files each 50 men deep. The Thebans preferred to fight on the left flank of the hoplite line. Here they would be facing the enemy right flank, the station of honour, where the enemy's best troops would be drawn up. A local victory here would ensure victory over the whole battlefield.

The élite *lochos* of the Theban army was the *Hieros lochos* or 'Sacred Band', which was also known as 'The City Company' because it was permanently stationed on the Kadmeia. These picked troops seem to have been the only standing army retained by the Thebans at first, but later passages seem to mention *epilektoi* in much larger numbers.

As well as the Boeotarchs we also hear of polemarchs in the individual cities of Boeotia. In Thebes there seem to have been three polemarchs. The precise functions of these magistrates have not yet been established and differentiated from those of the Boeotarchs, but they do seem to have been military officers. We hear of formations called *taxeis* above the *lochoi*, and it is possible that the polemarchs commanded them. Another officer mentioned in the texts is the 'Secretary' (*grammateus*) to the polemarchs. This officer seems to have acted as the Chief-of-Staff to the army. Before Leuctra we find the *grammateus* signalling to the officers of the army with a ribbon, or *tainia*—the symbol of victory—tied to a spear—see plate J.

The End of Greek Independence

The years between Mantineia in 362 and Chaironeia in 338 saw the rapid decline of Thebes as the premier power in Greece, and the failure of any other Greek state to seize power for herself. Into this power vacuum Philip of Macedon gradually inserted himself. Though the period was one of military weakness for most of the Greek city states, it was by no means one of inertia. Many attempts at military reform were made, but they were constantly hampered by the absence of funds in sufficient quantity to guarantee their successful implementation. Economic and social decline reduced the wealth of the citizens in the hoplite census class: meanwhile hoplite armour was becoming more complete and therefore more expensive, so fewer citizens were now able to serve. Under these circumstances the mercenary hoplite took on an importance even greater than he had enjoyed at the start of the 4th century, both in the armies of the states of Greece and also in Persian armies. The major problem of the employer was how to procure sufficient funds to keep an army in the field.

The Sacred War, 355–346 BC

The major political event of the period in the Greek mainland was the Sacred War. The Phocians refused to pay a crippling fine imposed on them by the Amphictyonic Council of Delphi for cultivating sacred land. The result was a long-drawn-out war with Thebes, lasting nearly ten years, which left both participants in a state of ruin.

Standing alone, the tiny army of the Phocians would have stood no chance against the Thebans and their allies; so the Phocian commander Philomelus devised a plan to enable him to expand the size of his army radically by using mercenaries.

Greek archers, such as this pair shown on the Nereid Monument from Xanthus, did not normally carry a shield. Above the archers a siege ladder has been placed against the battlements of an Asian city, and a party of hoplites are attempting to storm the ramparts under cover of the archers' arrows. (British Museum)

Philomelus obtained a subsidy from the Lakedaimonians, and doubled the sum by throwing in his own fortune. He then hired some mercenaries, supplied the pay for a thousand Phocians, seized Delphi, and confiscated the property of his political opponents. Eventually, however, Philomelus was compelled to lay hands on the sacred treasures of Delphi to finance the army. Now a larger force of mercenaries was raised by increasing the pay to half as much again as the normal rate in order to attract volunteers. More Phocians who were fit for active duty were enrolled in the army. This combination of mercenaries and maintained citizen *epilektoi* became the normal pattern for Greek armies in the later 4th century.

Plate K: The Battle of Tamynae, 349 BC

The Athenians had used the decline of Lakedaimon, then of Thebes, as an opportunity to rebuild their own power. Central to their imperial plans was the nearby island of Euboea, which they made repeated efforts to bring into an Athenian alliance. This necessitated numerous campaigns on the island. The first campaign in 357 freed the island from Theban domination. The Athenians were called in a second time in 349 by their ally Plutarch of Eretria. Philip of Macedon was trying to extend his influence to the island by establishing tyrants favourable to his cause in the various cities of Euboea, and was preparing to smuggle an army over to the island.

The Athenians sent over an army under their general Phocion, believing that the mass of the Euboeans would rally to their side. They did not, however, and Phocion soon found himself shut up on a crest of ground near the plains about Tamynae. Plutarch's rival, Callias of Chalcis, levied the troops of the Euboean League from all over the island; called upon Philip to send him reinforcements; and sent his brother Taurosthenes to bring over some of the Phocian mercenaries.

As the enemy approached the Athenian camp Plutarch rushed out with his mercenaries in an attempt to break out. His troops were soon dispersed and Plutarch took to flight. Unfortunately, the Athenian cavalry were also caught up in the panic. They had followed Plutarch out and had been dispersed. The division of the Euboeans which had just put Plutarch and the cavalry to flight now advanced on the ramparts, believing that the victory was already theirs. At this point Phocion sallied out of the camp with the main body of the Athenian infantry, and routed them. He then ordered the Athenian phalanx to halt and act as a rallying point for the dispersed cavalry and mercenaries, while he advanced against the main body of the Euboean army with the *epilektoi* alone. Phocion's subordinate Kleophanes managed to rally the Athenian cavalry, who returned to the battlefield in time to clinch the victory (Plut. *Vit. Phoc.* 13).

An Athenian funerary marble *lekythos* has been recovered dedicated to a cavalryman who almost certainly died in this campaign. He is shown riding

Cretan arrowheads are generally of cast bronze and about four inches long; they have a broad blade ending in two barbs, and a long tang which ends in a boss where it meets the blade. This example is Hellenistic, stamped with a ligature of the letters BE for Queen Berenike II of Egypt. (Manchester Museum, 1981.615)

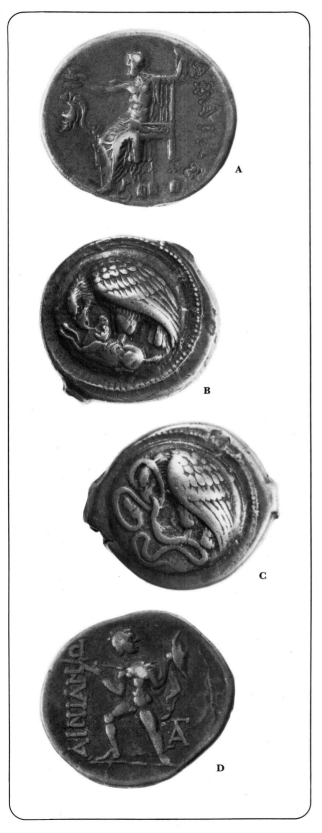

down a hoplite with a heifer's head as a shield device. This device is the badge of the Euboean League, so the cavalryman certainly died in battle fighting Euboean infantry, and the campaign of 349 is the only one in which we know the Athenian cavalry took part.

Plate K1: Athenian hamippos, *c.* 349 BC

Running behind the cavalryman is a light infantryman of the corps of *hamippoi*. The *hamippoi* were lightly armed infantry trained to fight alongside the cavalry; they would go into battle holding on to the tails and manes of the horses. *Hamippoi* were particularly useful in a straight cavalry fight, when they would hack at the enemy horsemen. A favourite trick was to slip underneath the enemy horse and rip its belly open with a dagger. Service in the *hamippoi* was evidently not for the faint-hearted. In his pamphlet *On the Duties of the Hipparch* (5.13, 9.7) Xenophon recommends that the Athenians should raise a corps of *hamippoi* from among the exiles and other foreigners in Athens who have special reason to be bitter against the enemy.

Hamippoi are first mentioned serving in the forces of the Syracusan tyrant Gelon (Hdt. 7.158), where his 2,000 cavalry are accompanied by an equal number of *hippodromoi psiloi* or 'psiloi who run alongside the cavalry'. *Hamippoi* are then found in the Boeotian army during the Peloponnesian War. It seems that when the Lakedaimonian army was reorganised some time after the battle of Mantineia in 418, the 600 Skiritai were not absorbed into the hoplite ranks of the *morai*, but were converted into *hamippoi* and fought alongside the 600 cavalry. After the battle of Leuctra in 371 the Skiritai achieved

(A) This stater is the major piece of evidence pointing to the existence of an Achaean League in the 360s. The reverse shows Zeus enthroned, with an eagle on his outstretched right hand; to the right, the triple-struck legend 'Of the Achaeans'; to the left, a Phrygian helmet. Cf. Plate I1. (B) Stater of the Eleians, *c.* 370. The splendid coinage of Elis, nearly all in large denominations, is clearly associated with the Olympic Games. The 4th-century school of Eleian engravers influenced coin-types in many other parts of Greece. The eagle's victim is variously identified as a ram or sheep, or, more probably, as a hare. (C) A second series of Eleian coins, *c.* 370, shows an eagle killing a snake. Both series show the device displayed on a hoplite shield, so we can guess that such shield devices were used by two different units of Eleian troops. Cf. Plate I2. (D) 4th century coin of the Aenianes used in reconstructing Plate J2. This Aenianian javelinman is using his stiff Thessalian hat as a makeshift shield. Later coins also show a similarly clad slinger, wearing a sword, with a pair of javelins stuck in the ground beside him. (British Museum)

Detail of a Panathenaic prize amphora, *c.* 530, showing the javelin thong in use; the thong imparted extra speed to the javelin, as well as rotation for stability in flight. Many of these vases, which were awarded to victorious athletes, show interesting details of Greek sporting life. Cf. Plate J2. (Leiden, Rijksmuseum van Oudheden, PC 8)

their independence from Lakedaimon; and at the second battle of Mantineia in 362 the Lakedaimonian cavalry fought on the right wing without the support of any *hamippoi* (Xen. *Hell.* 7.5.23).

Xenophon wrote his pamphlet *On the Duties of the Hipparch* in about 365, shortly before war broke out with Thebes. It seems that his recommendation that *hamippoi* be introduced into the Athenian army was implemented very soon afterwards. At the battle of Mantineia Diodorus (15.85.4) tells us that the Athenian cavalry on the left flank were defeated by their Theban opponents, not because of inferior mounts or horsemanship, but because of the greater numbers, better equipment and better tactical skill of the *psiloi* fighting for the Thebans. This implies that *psiloi*, in other words *hamippoi*, were fighting alongside the Athenian cavalry.

As no colours have survived on the *lekythos* of Kephisodotos we cannot restore the colours of the rider or of the *hamippos* with any certainty. The use of various shades of red for military uniform was becoming quite commonplace by now, however, so we shall not go too far wrong in restoring red. A second problem with this figure is that we do not know whether he is wearing a felt *pilos* hat or a bronze pilos-helmet. Here he has been shown with a felt hat.

The Athenian *hamippoi* drew pay. Aristotle (*Ath. Pol.* 49.1) tells us that the *hamippoi* and the *prodromoi* were inspected annually by the Athenian Council. If the Council found fault with any of the *hamippoi* they would be struck off the list and would lose their pay. Similarly, any of the *prodromoi* who were found to be unfit for service would be demoted back to the ranks of the line cavalry. This can be taken to imply that the *hamippoi* were recruited from among the poor and desperate men Xenophon recommended as being particularly suitable for service in the corps.

Plate K2: Athenian prodromos cavalryman, *c.* 349 BC

The *prodromoi* or 'Scouts' were a branch of the Athenian cavalry raised in the winter of 395/4 to replace the horse-archers, who were disbanded after the battle of Haliartos. The *prodromoi* took on the duties of scouts and couriers which the horse-archers had previously performed. They were internally recruited from among the tribal cavalry regiments, it seems; for Dexileos, who fell at Nemea in 394, and who seems to be a *prodromos*, is described in his funerary inscription as 'one of the five'. This is usually interpreted as indicating that each *phylē* of cavalry selected five of its best men to serve as *prodromoi*; so each hipparch would have a small troop of 25 at his disposal.

While Athenian reliefs showing cavalrymen invariably show them wearing cuirasses before 395/4, after that date they can be shown with or without body armour. It is possible that all those shown without cuirasses are *prodromoi*, but it is equally possible that in the first half of the 4th century the cuirass was rarely worn at all, even by the line cavalry. In the last half of the century, however, the cuirass is again shown in the majority of reliefs, now with the addition of groin-flaps, so we may be a little more certain that *prodromoi* are being shown. Another change which took place in the equipment was that the *petasos* hat and the 'petasos-helmet' were replaced at some point by the Boeotian helmet. This change is extremely difficult to date; but I would guess that the Athenian cavalry had adopted the Boeotian helmet by 362, and this is why the Theban horse who opposed them at the battle of Mantineia painted their helmets white to identify themselves in the mêlée.

As with the *hamippos*, colours are difficult to restore on this figure. One would expect uniform among the cavalry by this date and, indeed, Xenophon (*op. cit.* 1.23) reminds the *phylarchs* that they are entitled to arm the men in accordance with the regulations, compelling the men to pay for their arms afterwards. As much attention was devoted to the turnout of the cavalry on parades as was devoted to their performance on campaign. Demosthenes (4.35) tells us that as much money was spent annually on the Panathenaic and other festivals as would be required to fit out a naval expedition. One would expect the *prodromoi*, then, to put on quite a show.

In the relief the *prodromos* is shown using a javelin, and much attention was devoted to training the *prodromoi* in particular to be competent in the use of this weapon. Presumably, however, they also carried a cavalry spear.

Plate K3: Euboean hoplite, *c.* 349 BC
This figure can be identified from the shield device, a heifer's head shown cut off at the neck and turned towards the viewer, which was the badge of the Euboean League. The name Euboea means 'rich in cattle', and the heifer's head seems to make concious reference to the island's reputation. Coins of the Euboean League and of individual cities of the island show the head repeatedly during the period around 349, sometimes decked as for a sacrifice, and sometimes left plain. In plate K3 the head has been left plain to avoid difficulties of reconstructing the detail accurately.

The same difficulty has been encountered with this figure as with the other figures in plate K, and in K3 the colours are, again, uncertain. An additional problem is that we do not know whether the hoplite is a member of the hoplite levy of the Euboean League, as seems most probable, or whether he is one of the Phocian mercenaries hired by Taurosthenes.

By this time the Sacred War was reaching its conclusion and the Phocians were becoming ever more desperate to get their hands on money. Philomelus had been succeeded by his brothers Onomarchus and Phayllus, who had both been forced to plunder the treasures of Delphi. By this time the Phocians were reduced to melting down the offerings made by the Lydian kings 200 years or more previously, and plans were afoot to dig up the temples in search of hidden treasure underneath.

The mercenaries were not complaining, however, as long as the money kept coming, for their pay had now been increased to double the normal rate. Their newly acquired wealth was displayed in their arms. One group of these mercenaries later went to serve in Sicily under Timoleon, and we hear (Plut. *Vit. Tim.* 31.1) that their shields were decorated with murex-purple paint, gold, ivory and amber. So plate K3 has been restored bearing in mind the possibility that he might be a Phocian mercenary in Euboean service.

It is not absolutely certain whether the heifer's head is painted directly on to the shield, or whether it is placed on a painted 'medallion' surround, as we find in Macedonian shields of a slightly later period. There does seem to be a very light line cut on the shield, however, so a surround has been shown.

Drawing taken from a vase-painting, now lost, showing an athlete adorned with ribbons of victory. At the same time he receives the victor's crown in his hands. The significance of the headgear is unknown. (After Dar.-Sag. I, fig. 1335)

Another unusual feature of this figure is the helmet shape, which, although not unique in sculpture of this period, is extremely rare. It looks rather as if plate K3 is wearing a Corinthian helmet which has been 'modernised' into an open-faced helmet by cutting away the cheek and neck pieces.

Plate L1: Athenian hoplite, second half of the 4th Century BC

In the 360s Athenian funerary reliefs start to show hoplites wearing muscle-cuirasses and 'Phrygian' helmets. The muscle-cuirass is of the same shape as that worn by the Athenian cavalry earlier in the century, with a projection at the bottom edge covering the abdomen, except that the cuirass now has a couple of hinged bronze flaps at the shoulder. Sometimes the cuirass is worn with groin-flaps. Although the 'Phrygian' helmet now becomes the

Athenian funerary marble *lekythos* dedicated to Kephisodotos son of Konon of the deme Aithalidai. This example has the squat body-shape which the *lekythoi* increasingly took on in the 4th century. The figures in Plate K are based on this sculpture. (Athens, National Museum, 3620)

most common helmet form, older patterns continue to be worn alongside it. It might be the case that poorer citizens continued to use obsolete styles of helmet if they could not afford the latest style. Occasionally monuments show the Corinthian helmet still in use with the new muscle-cuirass. It is possible that this very traditional style of helmet was still worn only as a badge of rank by the *stratēgoi*, for busts depicting the Athenian generals of the 4th century invariably show the *stratēgoi* wearing such helmets.

Plate L1 is based on these late 4th century reliefs. Red colouring is preserved on the tunics and wrap-around *ephaptis* cloaks on a number of these Athenian grave monuments, including the marble *loutrophoros* of Polystratos son of Philopolis. Red is sometimes used as a base colour for crimson or purple, but it is more probable that plain red was used as the uniform colour.

The shield bears a letter '*alpha*' for Athens. American excavations in the Athenian Agora recently discovered a dump of lead tokens in a well some 70m away from the site of the Athenian Arsenal (John H. Kroll, *Hesperia* 46, 1977, pp. 141–6). These lead tokens show on one side an item of armour, such as a helmet or a cuirass, and on the reverse a letter giving the size. For example, there appear to have been four sizes of helmet, greave and cuirass available. A number of these tokens show hoplite shields with the letter '*alpha*' as a blazon. Though these tokens seem to be early Hellenistic in date rather than late Classical, the same shield blazon could well have been in use earlier on. The only literary evidence we have concerning Athenian shield decoration during this period is the statement (Plut. *Vit. Dem.* 20.2) that at the battle of Chaironeia Demosthenes had 'Good Luck!' written on his shield in gold. We are not told whether the words were written on the inside of the shield, or on the rim, or alongside a blazon.

The lead tokens imply state ownership and issue of arms and equipment in the Hellenistic period; but how far did the practice stretch back into the Classical period? As early as the 380s the banker Pasion donated a thousand shields to the state (Dem. 45.85), and this practice continued throughout the 4th century. Frequently the gifts were made by foreigners resident in Athens or by freed slaves in the hope of obtaining a grant of Athenian citizenship in return. In 369/8 an inventory of the Athenian Arsenal mentions over 1,000 shields in store, let alone any still on issue. As far as the Athenian state was concerned the main use of this armour was not to replace that owned by private citizens, but to expand the size of the hoplite force by providing arms for those too poor to afford them.

Athenian Army Reform

In the second half of the 4th century we start to hear of a 'division levy'. The idea of the 'division levy' seems to have been that only a proportion of the tribal *taxeis* would be sent out on campaign at any one time, to avoid the complete absence of age-groups over long periods. The cavalry also seem to have been divided into two divisions, each under its own hipparch, for the purposes of campaigning. These two divisions would rotate during the course of a campaign, as we know happened during the Euboean campaign of 349, one division going abroad while the other stayed in Attica. When the Athenians had succeeded in re-establishing their Empire, we frequently find one hipparch on duty in Attica and the other one in Lesbos.

Athenian *epilektoi* are first mentioned in 349 at Tamynae. Though there is no evidence to prove the point, we may perhaps assume that, as in other Greek states, maintenance was provided to enable them to serve. Aeschines (2.169) served in the *epilektoi* at Tamynae (presumably as an officer), where he won a crown for bravery.

The End of the Athenian Army

One last effort was made to expand the size of the hoplite force following the Greek defeat at the hands of Philip of Macedon at Chaironeia in 338. Now all citizens were to be trained as hoplites, and were given a shield by the state. The ephebe now served his first year in garrisons in the Piraeus, learning hoplite fighting, archery, javelin-throwing, and the use of the catapult. Then he received his spear, cloak and shield from the state, and completed a second year of hoplite service in the forts of Attica (Arist. *Ath. Pol.* 42.3). These changes are known as the Reforms of Lycurgus after the Athenian magistrate who implemented them.

In 301, however, the collaborating government of Athens, now occupied, made ephebic service voluntary. Registration of ephebes slumped from about 800 a year to 30; training was cut to one year; service in the garrisons and border forts was dispensed with; finally, lectures in philosophy were added to the military syllabus. In 278 the contingent sent by the Athenians to help the Aetolians repel the Galatian invasion numbered only 500 horse and 1,000 *epilektoi* (Paus. 10.20.5). We may suspect that the Athenian soldiery found certain elements of their new basic training of less practical use than others when they were faced by these Celtic barbarians.

Plate L2: Rhodian hoplite, end of the 4th Century BC

A lead token similar to those found in Athens has been discovered showing a shield bearing the device of a rose. Though this token is just a stray find without any provenance or date, we may presume that it served the same purpose as the Athenian tokens, is probably of a similar date, and originally came from Rhodes. In the beginning the island of Rhodes had been occupied by the three cities of Ialysos, Lindos and Kamiros; in 409 the island united, and the city of Rhodes was founded as a federal capital.

The rose was adopted as the symbol of Rhodes, and appears regularly on her coinage. This enables

In this Athenian relief a *hamippos* is shown running along behind the *prodromos* holding on to the horse's tail. The *petasos* hat hanging behind the horseman's neck presumably dates this relief prior to the introduction of the Boeotian helmet. Cf. Plate K1. (Musée du Louvre, 744.)

us to state that the lead token is Rhodian, and that the Rhodian shield device was a rose. All the other evidence on Rhodian equipment, unfortunately, is Hellenistic in date rather than Classical. The cuirass is based on an early Hellenistic sculpture, as is the tunic, but the colours are restored without any firm evidence.

Plate L3: Greek mercenary in Persian service, 330s BC

This figure is based on two figures of Greek mercenaries shown on the Alexander Mosaic from Pompeii. Rather peculiarly, both figures are shown with only a shield for defence and no other body armour. A few other helmeted heads are shown on the mosaic which could belong to Greek mercenaries, but there is no reason to think that the depiction of these two figures without helmets is not deliberate. On the Alexander Sarcophagus Greek mercenaries are also shown without body armour and sometimes without helmets. It may be, then, that Greek mercenaries in Persian service continued to wear the dress and armour of the 'light hoplite' which had been overtaken on the Greek mainland

Another Athenian relief shows a prodromos, *capped with a* petasos *and so dating to before the introduction of the Boeotian helmet, attacking a fallen enemy together with a* hamippos. *The weapon used by the* hamippos *is unclear; it could be a cudgel, or a Thessalian war-flail. (Budapest, Museum of Fine Arts, 4744)*

by the resurgence in popularity of body armour. Perhaps one factor in this was the intense heat in which the Greeks had to operate when in Persian service. Other features to notice in plate L3 are the long sword (which was diamond-shaped at the tip), which had replaced the Lakedaimonian short sword, and the thin head-band, which are both features of the later 4th century. The red tunic, shown on both Alexander Sarcophagus and Mosaic, had been the uniform of the mercenary ever since Xenophon's day.

Greek state contingents in Persian service

By the 350s mercenaries in Persian service were frequently not engaged for a campaign by individual contract, but were hired on loan from the armies of the Greek city states. The Persian Empire was finding it increasingly difficult to recruit mercenaries in sufficient numbers on the open market. On the other hand, the states of Greece were finding it increasingly difficult to provide financial support for their hoplite armies, which by now were composed of an ever-increasing proportion of maintained *epilektoi*. The obvious solution was for the Greek states to hire out their *epilektoi* to the Persians in time of peace. This relieved them of the financial burden of maintaining the *epilektoi*, and on the other hand it provided the Persians with

large numbers of already formed and trained hoplites serving under their own officers.

For their campaign to re-conquer Egypt in 343 the Persians managed to secure by these methods 1,000 Theban hoplites commanded by Lacrates and 3,000 Argive hoplites commanded by Nicostratos, in addition to 6,000 more hoplites raised in the Greek cities of Asia then under Persian control. The Rhodian Mentor was later appointed to the command of this last force.

Nicostratos, who was later to become ruler of Argos, had once been an epileptic. In order to be cured of 'the sacred disease' Nicostratos had taken himself off to the mad but brilliant Syracusan doctor Menecrates, who styled himself the 'Zeus of Medicine'. The good doctor agreed to offer his services but only on condition that, if cured, Nicostratos would become his disciple. On his recovery the hapless Nicostratos, who excelled in bodily strength, was compelled to dress as Herakles in a lion's skin and to carry a club, and to wait in attendance on Menecrates whenever summoned to do so. We find Nicostratus dressed in this garb even on campaign in Egypt in 343. Apart from this anecdotal scrap (of, it must be admitted, negligible value) there is no other literary evidence for the dress of Greek mercenaries in Persian service. As far as Nicostratos' Argive contingent is concerned, it is possible that white continued to be a distinctive colour of the Argives, as it had been in the 5th century; but it is more probable that by this time the uniform had changed to the more normal bronze and red.

Plate L4: Baggage-carrier
The hoplite would be accompanied on campaign by a slave, servant or attendant who would carry his baggage for him. These were generally considered to be cunning and dishonest fellows, and they appear in Greek comedy as a stock character. The hoplite would generally carry his own arms, especially his spear and shield, but all the baggage and rations would be loaded on to the servant. Over the shoulders the bedding-roll would be slung. Sometimes the bedding, or *strōmata*, would be tied on to the shield if carried by the hoplite himself. Plate L4 also shows what is probably a cooking pot tied on to the bedding roll. The square ration-basket, or *gulios*, which was made of wicker-work, is

suspended on one of the bedding straps. Staple rations consisted of barley-meal, which would be made up into bread, accompanied by onions and *tarichos* (fish or meat preserved by salting, drying, or smoking, and kept wrapped up in fig-leaves), and flavoured with salt mixed with thyme. At the start of a campaign it would be ordained how many days rations the citizen soldier had to provide himself with before setting out.

In time of peace the spear was kept in a case to prevent damage, and the shield would be hung on the wall. For cleaning or other occasional handling the shield was placed with its rim to the ground,

The Dexileos Monument. This magnificent funerary monument was discovered during excavations of the Athenian Sacred Way. The inscription runs: 'Dexileos, son of Lysanios, from Thorikos, born in the archonship of Teisandros [414/3], died in the archonship of Euboulides [394/3] at Corinth, one of the five cavalrymen'. Originally the sculpture of Dexileos would have had a bronze *petasos* and a long cavalry spear attached. Cf. Plate K2. (Athens, Keramaikos Museum, P 1130)

propped up by a special trestle. The bronze surface would be polished with oil to obtain the best shine. On campaign the shield would frequently be kept in its cover on the march to prevent tarnishing and the need for constant cleaning.

The Plates: Key Notes

(Fuller descriptions are given throughout the main body of the text, in historical sequence.)

Plate A represents Greek hoplites of around the 490s standing in front of a Greek fountain-house. *A1* shows a Lakedaimonian officer, based on a bronze statuette: the peculiar transverse plume is presumably a badge of rank. *A2* is a Samian hoplite. The shield device is based on a coin showing the lion-scalp badge of Samos on a hoplite shield. *A3* represents an Argive hoplite, based on texts and a vase painting. Most hoplites did not use uniform shield devices during this period, however, and *A4* bears the 'Leukopodes' badge of the Alkmaionid clan upon his shield.

Plate B shows the failure of a Greek expedition against the Thracians in the 440s. Thracian peltasts, shielded javelinmen such as *B1*, posed a great threat to the hoplite. *B2*, *B3*: Light-armed hoplites, called *ekdromoi*, were developed to chase the peltasts off. The cuirass was discarded and replaced with lighter fabric aprons and tunics.

The best cavalry in Greece came from Thessaly. *C1* is a Boeotian hoplite wearing the traditional Boeotian cap. He is shown trying to escape from a pair of Thessalian cavalrymen (*C2*, *C3*) who are each using a long cavalry spear called a *kamax*. The colours are all based on Athenian polychrome vases of around the 440s, and the scene might represent an incident during the Battle of Tanagra in 457.

Athens also expanded her cavalry force dramatically in 442. *Plate D* shows Athenian cavalry exercising in the north-west corner of the border fort of Phyle in about 430. *D1* shows the normal dress of an Athenian cavalryman, in hat and cuirass, shown on a large number of Athenian reliefs. *D2* wears a

Detail from the funerary relief of Panaitios, *c.* 395–390. The cavalryman, probably a *prodromos*, does not wear a cuirass. The baggy overfall of the tunic is typical for the period. Note the combination of *kamax*, with its small leaf-shaped head and long spear-butt, and pair of javelins. Cf. Plate K2. (Athens, National Museum, 884)

Coin of the Euboean League; the precise chronology of the coinage of the League is as yet uncertain. Some of these coins perhaps went to pay Taurosthenes' Phocian mercenaries. A heifer's head of just this type on the shield of Plate K3 allows us to identify him as a soldier of the Euboean League. (British Museum)

Detail of a marble *loutrophoros* showing Polystratos son of Philopolis. It is generally assumed that this Polystratos is a grandson of an earlier Polystratos active in 410/9, and so this relief is usually dated to the 390s. There is no reason why our Polystratos should not belong to a later generation of the same family, however, and a date in the 360s would fit the other archaeological evidence much better. Behind Polystratos stands a juvenile carrying the rest of his equipment. (Athens, National Museum, 3473). *Insert:* This anthropomorphic cheekpiece from a Phrygian helmet is of very similar shape to that shown on the *loutrophoros* of Polystratos: Cf. Plate LI. The Phrygian helmet is the subject of a new study by Mrs. J. Vokotopoulou in *Archäologischer Anzeiger*, 1982, pp. 497–520. (St. Germain-en-Laye, Musée des Antiquités Nationales, 4764)

Left: Athenian lead token, 20cm in diameter; there can be little doubt that these stamped lead tokens were an early form of 'chitty', probably hung on name-pegs when an item of armour had been issued out. (After *Hesperia* 46, 1977, pl. 40, 7) **Right:** Drawing of a Rhodian lead token, measuring 17cm in diameter, in the Numismatic Collection of the National Museum, Athens: this undoubtably had the same function as the Athenian examples. Cf. Plate L2. (After Arthur Engel, *BCH* 8, 1884, p. 21 & p. 6 nr. 222)

black cloak, which may be the mark of an ephebe or cadet, and a bronze helmet in the shape of a *petasos*-hat.

Plate E shows the defeat of the Athenian general Demosthenes' expedition to Aetolia in 426. *E1*, *E2* are Greek *psiloi*, or light infantrymen, while *E3* shows an Athenian hoplite using a state-issued shield. Probably, though, these shields were only issued for athletic competitions. All these figures are taken from vase-paintings.

Plate F represents hoplites of the Peloponnesian League invading Attica in 413: they are marching along a military road in southern Attica. *F1* is a Lakedaimonian hoplite, identifiable by his long hair and beard, and by his crimson and bronze uniform. *F2* is a Lakedaimonian officer: the plume seems to be a badge of rank. Allies of the Lakedaimonians, such as *F3*, a Tegean, copied Lakedaimonian uniform. (*Erratum*: Due to a misunderstanding, the cavalry in the background have been restored with hoplite shields, which were, of course, not used before the 270s.)

Plate G depicts hoplites of the Boeotian League at the Battle of Haliartos in 395, reconstructed from Boeotian vase paintings. *G2* wears boots, which seem to be a Boeotian peculiarity, and uses a shield with the snake badge of the Spartioi clan. *G3* may be a Theban, as his shield device is the club of

Herakles, the patron deity of Thebes.

In 382 the Lakedaimonians sent an allied army against Olynthus, and *Plate H* shows what the army may have looked like. *H1* is a Lakedaimonian cavalryman, based on reliefs of Castor and Pollux from Sparta. Lakedaimonian influence is clear in *H2*, a Macedonian infantryman based on a tombstone from Pella and a painting of a shield inside a Macedonian tomb. *H3* represents a Cretan archer and is based on a Cretan relief.

During the 360s Greek hoplites again adopted body armour. *Plate I* shows fighting at the Olympic Games of 364 involving Arcadian (*I1*), Eleian (*I2*), and Achaean picked troops, or *epilektoi*. These reconstructions are largely hypothetical.

Plate J shows the death of the Theban general Epameinondas (*J3*) at the Second Battle of Mantineia in 362. Other than the club shield device, nothing is known of Theban military dress during this period. *J1* and *J2* represent Thessalian

Drawing of a terracotta in the Louvre (S 1678 B) showing a hoplite with shield and helmet marching alongside a *skeuophoros* who is carrying his baggage. (After Dar.-Sag. IV, 2 fig. 6095)

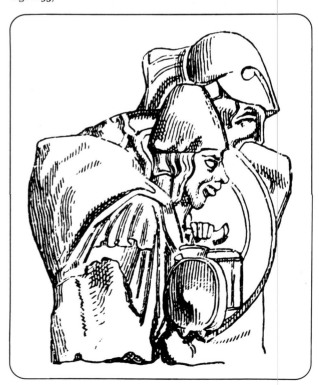

and Aenianian javelinmen, based on contemporary coins.

The figures shown in *Plate K* are all taken from an Athenian funerary monument commemorating a horseman who died in the Battle of Tamynae in 349. *K1* is an Athenian *hamippos*, a light-infantryman trained to go into battle with the cavalry, and *K2* is an Athenian *prodromos*, or 'Scout' cavalryman. *K3* can be identified as an infantryman in the service of the Euboean League from the heifer's head shield device, which appears on coins of the League.

Plate L shows an assortment of hoplites dating to the last years of Classical Greece. *L1* is an Athenian hoplite, reconstructed from Attic gravestones. The shield device is taken from a Hellenistic lead token, as is the shield device of *L2*, a Rhodian hoplite. *L3* shows a Greek mercenary hoplite in Persian service, taken from figures on the Alexander Mosaic. *L4* is a baggage-carrier, based on painted terracottas. The street scene is based on reconstructions of Athenian streets and houses.

Terracotta figure of a comic scallywag. For some reason this *skeuophoros* or 'baggage-carrier' has also been loaded down with the hoplite's sword. Traces of blue paint still adhere to the tunic and boots, and traces of yellow to the sword hilt. See Plate L4. (Berlin/DDR, Staatliche Museen zu Berlin, TC 7820)

Notes sur les planches en couleur

(Des descriptions plus complètes sont données dans le corps principal du texte anglais, mais comme il s'agit de longs passages intégrés, seul un bref résumé est possible ici.)

L'illustration A représente des *hoplites* grecs des années 490 environ devant une buvette grecque. **A1** montre un officier lacédémonien (d'après une statuette en bronze). Le bizarre plumet latéral est sans doute un insigne de grade. **A2**: *Hoplite* samien. L'emblème du bouclier est basé sur une pièce de monnaie montrant l'insigne de crinière de lion sur un bouclier d'hoplite. **A3** représente un *hoplite* argien, d'après des textes et des peintures sur vases. Cependant, la plupart des *hoplites* n'utilisaient pas d'emblèmes de bouclier identiques durant cette période et **A4** porte l'insigne 'Leukopodes' du clan Alkamaeonid sur son bouclier.

L'illustration B montre l'échec d'une expédition grecque contre les Thraces dans les années 440. Les *peltastes* thraces, fantassins armés de la pelta et protégés par un bouclier, (voir **B1**) constituaient le plus grand danger pour les *hoplites*. **B2**, **B3**: Des *hoplites* légers, appelés *ekdromoi*, furent formés pour lutter contre les *peltastes*. Leur cuirasse fut abandonnée et remplacée par un tablier et une tunique de tissu épais.

Les meilleurs cavaliers de Grèce venaient de la Thessalie. **C1** est un *hoplite* béotien portant la coiffe béotienne traditionnelle. Il tente ici de fuir deux cavaliers thessaliens, (**C2**, **C3**) qui portent une longue lance de cavalerie appelée '*kamax*'. Toutes les couleurs sont basées sur des vases athéniens polychromes d'environ 440 et l'illustration pourrait représenter un incident de la bataille de Tanagra, 457.

Athènes renforça aussi énormément sa cavalerie en 442. **L'illustration D** montre des cavaliers athéniennes s'exerçant dans le coin nord-ouest du fort de frontière de Phyle, aux environs de 430. **D1** montre le tenue normale d'un cavalier athénien, avec coiffe et cuirasse, présentée par un grand nombre de reliefs athéniens. **D2** porte un manteau noir, qui peut dénoter un *éphèbe* ou cadet, et un casque de bronze ayant la forme d'une coiffe *petasos*.

L'illustration E présente la défaite de l'expédition du général athénien Démosthène en Etolie en 426. **E1**, **E2** sont des *psiloi* ou fantassins légers grecs, et **E3** représente un *hoplite* athénien utilisant un bouclier distribué par l'état. Il est cependant probable que ces boucliers n'étaient distribués que pour les concours d'athlétisme. Tous ces personnages sont inspirés de peintures sur vases.

L'illustration F représente des *hoplites* de la Ligue du Péloponnèse envahissant l'Attique en 413; ils défilent sur une route militaire du sud du pays. **F1** est un *hoplite* lacédémonien, reconnaissable par ses longs cheveux et sa barbe, ainsi que par son uniforme cramoisi et bronze. **F2** est un officier lacédémonien; le plumet semble être un insigne de grade. Les alliés des lacédémoniens, tels que les tégéens (**F3**) copiaient l'uniforme des lacédémoniens.

L'illustration G présente des *hoplites* de la Ligue des Béotiens à la bataille d'Haliartos en 395, reconstitués d'après des peintures sur vases. **G2** porte des bottes, qui semblent particulières aux Béotiens, et utilise un bouclier portant l'insigne de serpent du clan spartioi. **G3** est peut-être thébain car l'emblème de son bouclier est la massue d'Héraclès, le dieu patron de Thèbes.

En 382, les Lacédémoniens envoyèrent une armée alliée contre Olynthe et **l'illustration H** montre l'aspect probable de cette armée. **H1** est un cavalier lacédémonien, d'après des reliefs de Castor et Pollux provenant de Sparte. L'influence lacédémonienne est évidente sur **H2**, fantassin macédonien, d'après une peinture tombale de Pella et une peinture de bouclier trouvé dans une tombe macédonienne. **H3** représente un archer crétois, d'après un relief crétois.

Durant les années 360, les hoplites grecs adoptèrent de nouveau l'armure. **L'illustration I** montre des combats aux Jeux Olympiques de 364 entre troupes sélectionnées arcadiennes (**I1**), éléennes (**I2**) et achéennes, ou *epilektoi*. Ces reconstitutions sont très hypothétiques.

L'illustration J montre la mort du général thébain Epaminonde (**J3**) à la seconde bataille de Mantinée en 362. A part l'emblème de la massue sur le bouclier, on ne sait rien de la tenue militaire thébaine durant cette période. **J1** et **J2** représentent des lanceurs de javelot thessaliens et énianiens, d'après des pièces de monnaie contemporaines.

Les personnages de **l'illustration K** sont tous tirés d'un monument funéraire athénien commémorant la mort d'un cavalier à la bataille de Tamynae en 349. **K1** est un *hamippos* athénien, fantassin léger formé pour aller à la bataille avec la cavalerie et **K2** est un *prodromos* athénien, ou cavalier éclaireur. **K3** est un fantassin au service de la Ligue Eubéenne, comme le montre l'emblème de son bouclier, une tête de génisse, qui se trouve sur les pièces de monnaie de la Ligue.

L'illustration L montre divers *hoplites* des dernières années de l'âge classique de la Grèce. **L1** est un *hoplite* athénien, reconstitué d'après des pierres tombales attiques. L'emblème provient d'un jeton hellénistique en plomb, de même que l'emblème de bouclier de **L2**, qui représente un hoplite rhodien. **L3** est un *hoplite* mercenaire grec au service des Perses, tiré de personnages de la Mosaïque d'Alexandre. **L4** est un porteur de bagages, tiré de terres cuites peintes. La scène de rue est basée sur des reconstitutions des rues et des maisons athéniennes.

Farbtafeln

(Ausführlichere Beschreibungen finden sich im englischen Textteil; da es sich um längere eingebaute Passagen handelt, können hier nur kurze Zusammenfassungen gegeben werden.)

Tafel A zeigt griechische Hopliten in den 490er Jahren vor eine griechischen Badehaus. **A1** ist ein lakedämonischer Offizier, nach einer Bronzestatuette. Die merkwürdige Querfeder ist vermutlich ein Rangabzeichen. **A2** zeigt einen samischen Hopliten. Der Schild basiert auf einer Münze mit dem Löwenfellabzeichen von Samos auf einem Hoplitenschild. **A3** ist ein Hoplit aus Argos nach Texten und Vasenmalereien. Die meisten Hopliten hatten in dieser Periode jedoch keine einheitlichen Schilde, und **A4** zeigt einen Kämpfer mit dem 'Leukopodes'-Abzeichen der Alkmäoniden auf seinem Schild.

Tafel B zeigt die Niederlage einer griechischen Expedition gegen die Thraker in den 440er Jahren. Thrakische Peltasten, schildtragende Soldaten mit Wurfspeeren wie in **B1**, stellten eine ernsthafte Bedrohung für die Hopliten dar. **B2** und **B3** zeigen leicht bewaffnete Hopliten, sogenannte ekdromoi, die die Peltasten abwehren sollten. Der Kürass wurde abgeworfen und durch leichtere Schürzen und Tuniken aus Stoff ersetzt.

Die besten berittenen Streiter Griechenlands kamen aus Thessalien. **C1** zeigt einen böotischen Hopliten mit der traditionellen böotischen Kappe. Er wird auf der Flucht vor zwei thessalischen Reitern dargestellt (**C2**, **C3**), die beide einen langen Reiterspeer (kamax) benutzen. Die Farben beruhen auf mehrfarbigen athenischen Vasen aus den 440er Jahren, und die Szene stellt vielleicht einen Vorfall aus der Schlacht von Tanagra (457) dar.

Athen erweiterte seine Rettertruppen im Jahr 442. **Tafel D** zeigt athenische Reiter bei Übungen im Nordwesten der Grenzfestung von Phyle um 430, **D1** zeigt die normale Bekleidung für athenische Reiter, mit Kopfbedeckung und Kürass, wie auf zahlreichen athenischen Reliefs dargestellt. **D2** trägt einen schwarzen Mantel, vielleicht das Erkennungszeichen eines Epheben oder Kadetten, und einen Bronzehelm in der Form eines Petasos-Huts.

Tafel E zeigt die Niederlage des Feldzugs des athenischen Generals Demosthenes in Ätolien im Jahr 426. **E1** und **E2** sind griechische psiloi (leichte Reiter), **E3** ist ein athenischer Hoplit mit einem vom Staat ausgegebenen Schild. Diese Schilder wurden allerdings voraussichtlich für athletische Wettkämpfe ausgegeben. All diese Figuren stammen von Vasenmalereien.

Tafel F zeigt Hopliten beim Einmarsch des Peloponnesischen Bunds in Attika im Jahr 413: Sie marschieren über eine Militärstrasse im südlichen Attika. **F1** ist ein lakedämonischer Hoplit, erkenntlich an seinen langen Haaren und dem Bart sowie an der kermesinroten und bronzenen Uniform. **F2** ist ein lakedämonischer Offizier; der Kamm ist anscheinend ein Rangabzeichen. Verbündete der Lakedämonier, wie der Tegäer (**F3**), kopierten die Lakedämonische Uniform.

Tafel G zeigt Hopliten des Böotischen Bunds bei der Schlacht von Haliartos im Jahr 395, nach böotischen Vasenmalereien. **G2** trägt Stiefel, offenbar eine böotische Eigenheit, und benutzt einen Schild mit dem Schlangenabzeichen der Sippe der Spartioi. **G3** ist möglicherweise ein Thebaner, da sein Schild die Keule des Herakles trägt, das thebanische Schutzgotts.

Im Jahr 382 schickten die Lakedämonier eine Bundesarmee gegen Olynthus, und **Tafel H** zeigt, wie die Streiter möglicherweise aussahen. **H1** ist ein lakedämonischer Reiter, nach den Reliefs des Kastor und Pollux in Sparta. Lakedämonischer Einfluss zeigt sich auch bei **H2**, einem mazedonischen Fusssoldaten nach einem Grabstein in Pella und einem Schildgemälde in einem mazedonischen Grab. **H3** ist ein kretischer Bogenschütze nach einem kretischen Relief.

Während der 360er Jahre übernahmen die griechischen Hopliten wiederum Körperpanzerung. **Tafel I** zeigt Kämpfe bei den Olympischen Spielen des Jahres 364, darunter arkadische (**I1**) und achäische epilektoi oder ausgewählte Truppen. Diese Rekonstruktionen beruhen weitgehend auf Hypothesen.

Tafel J zeigt den Tod des thebanischen Generals Epameinondas (**J3**) bei der zweiten Schlacht von Mantineia im Jahr 362. Bis auf den keulenschild ist über die militärische Ausrüstung der Thebaner dieser Periode nichts bekannt. **J1** und **J2** sind thessalische und änianische Speerwerfer nach zeitgenössischen Münzen.

Die Figuren auf **Tafel K** stammen alle aus einem athenischen Grabdenkmal für einen Reiter, der in der Schlacht von Tamynä im Jahr 349 fiel. **K1** ist ein athenischer Hamippos, ein leichter Fusssoldat, der mit den Reitern in die Schlacht zog; **K2** ist ein athenischer prodromos oder Späher, ebenfalls berritten. **K3** ist offenbar ein Reiter im Dienst des Euböischen Bunds (ein solcher Färsenkopf wie auf dem Schild findet sich auf Münzen der Bundesstaaten).

Tafel L zeigt verschiedene Hopliten bis hin zu den letzten Jahren des klassischen Hellas. **L1** ist ein athenischer Hoplit nach attischen Grabmalen. Der Schild ist nach einem hellenistischen Bleipfand entworfen, ebenso wie der Schild des rhodischen Hopliten **L2**. **L3** zeigt einen griechischen Hopliten, der als Söldner im persischen Dienst stand, nach Figuren des Alexander-Mosaiks. **L4** ist ein Lastträger nach bemalten Terrakottas. Die Strassenszene basiert auf Rekonstruktionen von athenischen Strassen und Häusern.